U.S. Military's Role in Combatting Colombia's Drug Trafficking and Insurgencies

Copyright Page

TITLE: U.S. Military's Role in Combatting Colombia's Drug Trafficking and Insurgencies

1ST Edition

Table of Contents

U.S. Military's Role in Combatting Colombia's Drug Trafficking and Insurgencies

By Roberto Miguel Rodriguez

Chapter 1: U.S. Military and Financial Aid to Colombia to Combat Drug Trafficking and Insurgent Groups

History of U.S. involvement in Colombia

The history of U.S. involvement in Colombia is a complex and multifaceted one, characterized by both military and financial support aimed at combating drug trafficking and insurgent groups. This subchapter explores the various ways in which the United States has contributed to Colombia's efforts in addressing these pressing issues.

One key aspect of U.S. involvement has been the provision of military aid and training programs for the Colombian armed forces. Recognizing the importance of a strong and capable military in combating drug trafficking and insurgency, the United States has supported Colombia through the training of its armed forces, enabling them to effectively address these challenges.

Financial aid has also played a crucial role in Colombia's counter-narcotics operations. The United States has provided significant financial assistance to support Colombia's efforts in interdicting drug shipments, disrupting money laundering networks, and dismantling drug cartels. This aid has not only helped Colombia in its fight against drug trafficking but has also contributed to the overall security and stability of the region.

Moreover, the U.S. military has provided valuable assistance in intelligence gathering and surveillance in Colombia. Through the sharing of intelligence and advanced surveillance technology, the United States has helped Colombian authorities in tracking and apprehending drug traffickers and insurgent groups.

In addition to military support, the United States has also extended financial aid for Colombian law enforcement agencies involved in drug interdiction. This support has enabled Colombian authorities to enhance their capacity to intercept drug shipments and carry out successful operations against drug traffickers.

Recognizing the importance of addressing the root causes of drug addiction, the United States has provided financial aid for Colombian programs focused on drug addiction prevention and treatment. By supporting these initiatives, the United States aims to reduce the demand for illicit drugs and promote healthier communities.

Furthermore, U.S. military aid has been instrumental in supporting Colombian efforts in border security and drug trafficking prevention. Through the provision of resources and training, the United States has helped Colombia enhance its border control measures, preventing the flow of drugs across its borders.

Lastly, the United States has contributed financially to Colombian programs aimed at alternative livelihoods and economic development in regions affected by drug trafficking and insurgent groups. By promoting economic opportunities and sustainable development, these programs seek to address the underlying issues that fuel drug trafficking and insurgency.

In conclusion, the history of U.S. involvement in Colombia demonstrates the comprehensive support provided by the United States, encompassing various aspects such as military aid, financial assistance, intelligence sharing, and capacity building. This support reflects the commitment of the United States in partnering with Colombia to combat drug trafficking and insurgent groups, ultimately contributing to the security and prosperity of both nations.

Evolution of U.S. military assistance in Colombia

The Evolution of U.S. Military Assistance in Colombia

Introduction:

The battle against drug trafficking and insurgent groups has been a long-standing challenge for Colombia. Throughout the years, the United States has played a crucial role in supporting Colombia's efforts to combat these issues. This subchapter explores the evolution of U.S. military assistance in Colombia, highlighting the various areas in which support has been provided.

U.S. Military and Financial Aid to Colombia to Combat Drug Trafficking and Insurgent Groups:

The United States has been a key partner to Colombia in its fight against drug trafficking and insurgent groups. Over the years, financial aid has been provided to strengthen the Colombian armed forces and law enforcement agencies. This support has enabled Colombia to enhance its capacities in areas such as intelligence gathering, surveillance, and border security.

U.S. Military Training Programs for Colombian Armed Forces:

The U.S. military has played a critical role in training and equipping Colombian armed forces. Through specialized training programs, Colombian troops have been able to enhance their skills in counter-narcotics operations and insurgent group neutralization. These training programs have been instrumental in improving Colombia's overall military capabilities.

Financial Aid for Colombian Counter-Narcotics Operations:

Financial assistance from the United States has been essential in supporting Colombian counter-narcotics operations. This aid has enabled Colombia to invest in advanced technology, equipment, and resources necessary for effective drug interdiction. Additionally, financial support has been provided to programs focused on drug addiction prevention and treatment.

U.S. Military Support for Colombian Efforts to Combat Insurgent Groups:

In addition to combating drug trafficking, Colombia has faced significant challenges from insurgent groups. The United States has extended its support to Colombia's efforts in neutralizing these groups. U.S. military assistance has included intelligence sharing, training, and equipment to enhance Colombia's capabilities in countering insurgent activities.

Financial Assistance for Colombian Law Enforcement Agencies in Drug Interdiction:

In the fight against drug trafficking, Colombian law enforcement agencies have received financial aid from the United States. This assistance aims to strengthen their capacities in drug interdiction, intelligence gathering, and dismantling money laundering networks associated with drug cartels.

Conclusion:

The evolution of U.S. military assistance in Colombia has been crucial in combating drug trafficking and insurgent groups. Through financial aid, training programs, and equipment support, the United States has played a significant role in enhancing Colombia's ability to tackle these issues. The partnership between the two nations continues to evolve, with a focus on alternative livelihoods, economic development, and sustainable solutions in regions affected by drug trafficking and insurgent groups. This collaboration serves as a testament to the effectiveness of international cooperation in addressing complex challenges.

Financial aid from the U.S. for Colombian security forces

In the battle against drug trafficking and insurgent groups in Colombia, the United States has played a crucial role by providing extensive financial aid to Colombian security forces. This support has been instrumental in strengthening the capabilities of the Colombian armed forces, law enforcement agencies, and intelligence agencies, enabling them to effectively combat the scourge of drug trafficking and insurgency.

One of the key areas where the U.S. has provided financial aid is through military training programs for the Colombian armed forces. These programs focus on enhancing the skills of Colombian military personnel in counter-narcotics operations, intelligence gathering, and surveillance. By equipping Colombian forces with state-of-the-art training and equipment, the U.S. has helped them to effectively identify and neutralize drug cartels and insurgent groups.

Financial assistance has also been directed towards Colombian law enforcement agencies involved in drug interdiction efforts. This support has enabled the Colombian authorities to strengthen their capabilities in combating money laundering networks associated with drug trafficking. By disrupting these networks, Colombia has been able to severely cripple the financial resources of drug cartels, making it harder for them to operate.

Additionally, the U.S. has provided financial aid for programs aimed at drug addiction prevention and treatment in Colombia. Recognizing the importance of addressing the root causes of drug trafficking, these programs focus on providing support for individuals affected by drug addiction, as well as promoting alternative livelihoods and economic development in regions impacted by drug trafficking and insurgency.

Furthermore, the U.S. has extended its financial assistance to support Colombian efforts in border security and drug trafficking prevention. By providing resources for the enhancement of border control measures, the U.S. has helped Colombia in preventing the flow of drugs across its borders and disrupting the activities of drug cartels.

In conclusion, the financial aid provided by the U.S. to Colombian security forces has been pivotal in the battle against drug trafficking and insurgent groups. Through military training programs, support for law enforcement agencies, intelligence gathering, and surveillance, as well as initiatives focused on drug addiction prevention and economic development, the U.S. has significantly contributed to Colombia's efforts to combat these threats. This assistance has not only strengthened the capabilities of Colombian security forces but has also helped to disrupt the financial networks of drug cartels and promote stability and progress in regions affected by drug trafficking and insurgency.

U.S. military's strategic objectives in Colombia

The United States' military involvement in Colombia has been instrumental in combating drug trafficking and insurgent groups within the country. This subchapter aims to shed light on the strategic objectives that the U.S. military has pursued in its collaboration with Colombia. By understanding these objectives, diplomats and historians can gain insights into the U.S.'s role in Colombia's battle against drug trafficking and insurgencies.

One of the primary objectives of the U.S. military in Colombia has been to provide financial aid to support Colombian counter-narcotics operations. Through these efforts, the U.S. aims to disrupt drug trafficking networks and reduce the flow of illicit drugs into the United States. Financial assistance has also been extended to Colombian law enforcement agencies involved in drug interdiction, enabling them to enhance their capabilities and effectiveness in combating drug-related crimes.

Furthermore, the U.S. military has played a crucial role in providing intelligence gathering and surveillance support to Colombia. This assistance has helped Colombian authorities in identifying and targeting key individuals and organizations involved in drug trafficking and insurgent activities. By bolstering Colombia's intelligence capabilities, the U.S. aims to improve the overall security situation in the region.

In addition to intelligence support, the U.S. military has focused on training programs for the Colombian armed forces. These programs aim to enhance the professionalism, capacity, and capabilities of Colombian security forces, enabling them to effectively counter insurgent groups and drug cartels. This collaboration has strengthened the partnership between the two nations and facilitated the exchange of knowledge and expertise.

Financial aid has also been directed towards programs focused on drug addiction prevention and treatment. Recognizing the importance of addressing the demand side of the drug problem, the U.S. military has supported Colombian initiatives aimed at combating drug addiction and providing rehabilitation services to affected individuals.

Moreover, the U.S. military has provided assistance in border security and drug trafficking prevention. By supporting Colombian efforts to secure its borders, the U.S. aims to prevent the movement of drugs and illicit activities across international boundaries. This collaboration has been crucial in disrupting the operations of drug cartels and insurgent groups that exploit porous borders.

Finally, the U.S. has extended financial aid to Colombian programs focused on alternative livelihoods and economic development in regions affected by drug trafficking and insurgencies. By promoting economic opportunities and sustainable development, the U.S. aims to address the root causes of drug production and insurgent activities, ultimately contributing to long-term stability and prosperity in Colombia.

In summary, the U.S. military's strategic objectives in Colombia encompass a range of areas, including financial aid for counter-narcotics operations, training programs for Colombian armed forces, intelligence gathering and surveillance, and support for border security and economic development initiatives. Through these efforts, the U.S. aims to combat drug trafficking, dismantle insurgent groups, and contribute to the overall stability and security of Colombia.

Evaluation of the effectiveness of U.S. military and financial aid

The Battle for Colombia: U.S. Military's Role in Combating Drug Trafficking and Insurgent Groups

Introduction:

The United States has played a significant role in providing military and financial aid to Colombia to combat drug trafficking and insurgent groups. This subchapter aims to evaluate the effectiveness of such assistance, discussing the various aspects of U.S. involvement and its impact on Colombian efforts to address these pressing challenges. Addressed to diplomats and historians, this analysis provides a comprehensive understanding of the outcomes and implications of U.S. military and financial aid in Colombia.

U.S. Military Training Programs for Colombian Armed Forces:

One of the key components of U.S. assistance has been the provision of military training programs for the Colombian armed forces. These programs have greatly enhanced the capabilities and professionalism of

Colombian troops, enabling them to effectively combat drug traffickers and insurgent groups. The training has resulted in improved operational tactics, intelligence gathering, and overall effectiveness in countering these threats.

Financial Aid for Colombian Counter-Narcotics Operations:

The financial aid provided by the United States has been instrumental in strengthening Colombian counter-narcotics operations. The funding has supported the procurement of advanced equipment, technology, and resources necessary for effective drug interdiction. Additionally, financial assistance has facilitated the development of intelligence networks and surveillance capabilities, enabling Colombian authorities to better track and disrupt drug trafficking operations.

U.S. Military Support for Colombian Efforts to Combat Insurgent Groups:

In the battle against insurgent groups, U.S. military support has been pivotal in bolstering Colombian efforts. Through joint operations, intelligence sharing, and logistical support, the United States has helped Colombian forces in their fight against these extremist organizations. The collaboration between the two nations has resulted in significant setbacks for insurgent groups, weakening their infrastructure and reducing their capacity to carry out attacks.

Financial Assistance for Colombian Law Enforcement Agencies in Drug Interdiction:

To enhance Colombian law enforcement agencies' capacity to combat drug trafficking, the United States has provided financial aid. This has facilitated the strengthening of law enforcement institutions, including improving their capabilities in drug interdiction, money laundering prevention, and dismantling drug cartels. The financial assistance has also supported training initiatives and the implementation of advanced technologies to enhance the effectiveness of Colombian law enforcement agencies.

Conclusion:

The evaluation of U.S. military and financial aid to Colombia reveals a substantial positive impact on the country's efforts to combat drug trafficking and insurgent groups. Through military training programs, financial aid, intelligence support, and collaboration in various areas, the United States has significantly contributed to Colombia's progress in addressing these challenges. However, continuous evaluation and refinement of these aid programs are necessary to ensure ongoing effectiveness and adaptability to evolving threats. The collaboration between the United States and Colombia remains crucial in the battle against drug trafficking and insurgent groups, fostering a safer and more stable Colombia while protecting U.S. interests in the region.

Chapter 2: U.S. Military Training Programs for Colombian Armed Forces

Overview of U.S. military training programs in Colombia

The U.S. military has played a significant role in supporting Colombia's efforts to combat drug trafficking and insurgent groups. Through various training programs, financial aid, and assistance, the United States has been a key partner in helping Colombia address these persistent challenges.

One of the major areas of focus for U.S. military support is the training of Colombian armed forces. The U.S. military provides extensive training and education programs to enhance the capabilities of Colombian soldiers in combating drug traffickers and insurgent groups. This includes specialized training in counterinsurgency tactics, intelligence gathering, and border security. By equipping Colombian armed forces with the necessary skills and knowledge, the U.S. military aims to build a stronger and more effective fighting force.

Financial aid is another crucial aspect of U.S. support for Colombia's counter-narcotics operations. The United States provides substantial financial assistance to help fund Colombian efforts in drug interdiction, intelligence gathering, and surveillance. This financial aid enables Colombia to acquire modern technology, equipment, and resources necessary to disrupt drug trafficking networks effectively.

Furthermore, U.S. military assistance extends to supporting Colombian law enforcement agencies in drug interdiction. Through financial aid, training, and cooperation, the United States helps strengthen Colombian law enforcement capabilities, enabling them to better combat drug trafficking and dismantle criminal networks.

In addition to addressing drug trafficking, the U.S. military also aids Colombian efforts to combat insurgent groups. This includes financial assistance for intelligence gathering and surveillance, which helps monitor and neutralize insurgent activities. Moreover, U.S. military aid supports Colombian efforts in border security, preventing the flow of drugs and weapons across borders.

Financial aid from the United States also focuses on disrupting money laundering networks associated with drug trafficking. By targeting the financial infrastructure that sustains drug cartels, the U.S. military aids Colombian efforts to dismantle and neutralize these criminal organizations.

Recognizing the need for long-term solutions, the United States also provides financial aid for Colombian programs aimed at drug addiction prevention and treatment. By supporting prevention and treatment initiatives, the U.S. military contributes to reducing demand for illicit drugs and addresses the root causes of drug abuse.

Finally, U.S. military assistance extends to supporting Colombian programs focused on alternative livelihoods and economic development in regions affected by drug trafficking and insurgent groups. By promoting economic opportunities in these areas, the United States aims to reduce the appeal and influence of drug cartels and insurgent groups.

Overall, the U.S. military's training programs and financial aid in Colombia play a crucial role in combating drug trafficking and insurgent groups. By strengthening Colombian armed forces, enhancing law enforcement capabilities, and supporting long-term solutions, the United States contributes to the stability and security of both nations.

Objectives and focus of U.S. military training

The United States has played a significant role in supporting Colombia's efforts to combat drug trafficking and insurgent groups. As part of this assistance, the U.S. military has provided extensive training programs to the Colombian armed forces. This subchapter explores the objectives and focus of these training initiatives, shedding light on the motivations and strategies behind U.S. involvement in Colombia's security landscape.

At its core, the U.S. military training aims to enhance the capabilities and professionalism of the Colombian armed forces. By equipping Colombian soldiers with advanced skills and knowledge, the United States seeks to bolster their ability to tackle drug trafficking networks and insurgent groups effectively. The primary objective is to build a strong and capable defense force that can efficiently counter these threats while upholding human rights and the rule of law.

One of the key focuses of U.S. military training programs is intelligence gathering and surveillance. By improving the Colombian military's capacity in this area, the U.S. aims to support intelligence-led operations against drug traffickers and insurgent organizations. This includes training in the use of advanced surveillance technologies, data analysis, and intelligence sharing mechanisms, all aimed at disrupting criminal networks and enhancing the effectiveness of counter-narcotics operations.

The U.S. military training also emphasizes border security and drug trafficking prevention. Given Colombia's geographical location as a major transit point for drug shipments, securing its borders is central to combating drug trafficking effectively. The training provided by the U.S. equips Colombian forces with the skills and knowledge necessary to detect and intercept drug shipments, thereby disrupting the flow of narcotics and reducing their impact on both Colombian and international societies.

Additionally, the U.S. military training programs focus on supporting Colombian efforts to dismantle drug cartels and disrupt money laundering networks. By enhancing the Colombian armed forces' capabilities in these areas, the United States aims to undermine the financial infrastructure of drug trafficking organizations, weakening their influence and operational capacity.

Furthermore, U.S. military assistance extends beyond traditional security measures. Financial aid is directed towards supporting Colombian programs aimed at drug addiction prevention and treatment, as well as alternative livelihoods and economic development in regions affected by drug trafficking and insurgent groups. By addressing the root causes of these issues, the U.S. aims to create sustainable solutions that reduce the allure of illicit activities and promote stability and prosperity in Colombia.

In conclusion, the objectives and focus of U.S. military training in Colombia are multifaceted. They encompass enhancing the capabilities of the Colombian armed forces, improving intelligence gathering and surveillance, strengthening border security, dismantling drug cartels, disrupting money laundering networks, and supporting comprehensive programs aimed at reducing drug addiction and fostering economic development. By addressing these various aspects, the United States aims to contribute to Colombia's long-term security, stability, and prosperity.

Training methods and curriculum

Training methods and curriculum play a crucial role in the success of any military operation. In the context of the U.S. military's role in combating drug trafficking and insurgent groups in Colombia, the training programs implemented for the Colombian armed forces are of utmost importance. This subchapter will delve into the various training methods and curriculum employed by the U.S. military to support Colombian efforts in this battle.

The U.S. military's training programs for the Colombian armed forces are designed to enhance their capabilities in countering drug trafficking and insurgent groups effectively. These programs focus on building the necessary skills, knowledge, and tactics required to carry out operations successfully. This includes training in areas such as counter-narcotics operations, border security, intelligence gathering, surveillance, and law enforcement techniques.

The curriculum for these training programs is carefully crafted to address the unique challenges faced by Colombian forces. It incorporates lessons learned from previous experiences, both in Colombia and other regions combating similar threats. The curriculum covers a wide range of topics, including tactics for interdicting drug shipments, strategies for dismantling and neutralizing drug cartels, methods for disrupting money laundering networks, and approaches for preventing drug addiction and promoting alternative livelihoods in affected regions.

Furthermore, financial aid is provided to Colombian counter-narcotics operations to support these training programs. This assistance allows for the procurement of necessary equipment, infrastructure development, and logistical support. The financial aid also helps in the establishment of specialized units and the enhancement of intelligence capabilities, ensuring a comprehensive approach to combating drug trafficking and insurgent groups.

The U.S. military's support for Colombian efforts in training and capacity-building extends beyond the armed forces. Financial assistance is also provided to Colombian law enforcement agencies involved in drug interdiction. This aid helps in the training of personnel, the acquisition of modern equipment, and the strengthening of institutional capacities.

In conclusion, the U.S. military's training methods and curriculum are crucial components of their support to Colombia in combating drug trafficking and insurgent groups. These programs provide the Colombian armed forces with the necessary skills and knowledge to carry out successful operations. Additionally, financial aid plays a vital role in supporting these training programs and enhancing the capabilities of Colombian forces. Through these efforts, the U.S. military aims to contribute to the overall stability and security of Colombia, as well as the region as a whole.

Impact of U.S. military training on Colombian armed forces

The Battle for Colombia: U.S. Military's Role in Combating Drug Trafficking and Insurgent Groups

Introduction:

The United States has played a significant role in supporting Colombia's efforts to combat drug trafficking and insurgent groups. One crucial aspect of this support is the provision of military training to the Colombian armed forces. This subchapter aims to explore the impact of U.S. military training on the Colombian armed forces, highlighting its significance in enhancing Colombia's ability to address security challenges effectively.

Enhanced Capabilities:

The U.S. military's training programs have resulted in a significant enhancement of the Colombian armed forces' capabilities. Through these programs, Colombian soldiers have gained valuable skills, including advanced tactics, intelligence gathering, and surveillance techniques. This has led to improved operational effectiveness in countering drug trafficking and insurgent groups, ultimately contributing to a more secure Colombia.

Improved Border Security and Drug Trafficking Prevention:

U.S. military aid has been instrumental in supporting Colombian efforts to strengthen border security and prevent drug trafficking. Training programs focused on border surveillance and interdiction have equipped Colombian forces with the necessary skills to detect and disrupt drug smuggling activities. This has had a direct impact on reducing the flow of drugs across Colombia's borders, thereby curbing the reach of drug cartels.

Dismantling Drug Cartels:

Colombia has long been plagued by powerful drug cartels that pose a threat to national security. U.S. military assistance has played a pivotal role in dismantling and neutralizing these criminal networks. Training programs have provided Colombian forces with the expertise to target and apprehend high-value cartel members, leading to significant blows against the drug trade and its associated violence.

Promoting Alternative Livelihoods and Economic Development:

In addition to military training, the United States has provided financial aid to Colombian programs focused on alternative livelihoods and economic development in regions affected by drug trafficking and insurgent groups. By supporting initiatives that promote legal economic activities, such as agriculture and tourism, the U.S. has helped create opportunities for local communities, making them less susceptible to the influence of drug cartels and insurgent groups.

Conclusion:

The impact of U.S. military training on the Colombian armed forces cannot be overstated. It has resulted in enhanced capabilities, improved border security, dismantling of drug cartels, and the promotion of alternative livelihoods and economic development. By addressing the security challenges posed by drug trafficking and insurgent groups, this collaboration has significantly contributed to a safer and more prosperous Colombia. The continued support and cooperation between the United States and Colombia remain crucial in achieving lasting peace and stability in the region.

Challenges and criticisms of U.S. military training programs

The Battle for Colombia: U.S. Military's Role in Combating Drug Trafficking and Insurgent Groups

Introduction:

As diplomats and historians delve into the complex relationship between the United States and Colombia, it is essential to examine the challenges and criticisms surrounding U.S. military training programs. These programs have played a significant role in supporting Colombian armed forces, countering drug trafficking, and combating insurgent groups. However, they have not been without their fair share of obstacles and critiques.

1. Limited effectiveness of training programs:

One of the key challenges faced by U.S. military training programs is their limited effectiveness in achieving long-term goals. Critics argue that the training provided by the U.S. military may not always translate into sustainable capabilities for the Colombian armed forces. This raises concerns about the efficiency and value of the financial aid provided.

2. Human rights concerns:

Another criticism is the human rights record of Colombian armed forces that have received U.S. military training. While the programs aim to enhance professionalism and adherence to international norms, reports of human rights abuses by trained personnel have emerged. This raises questions about the adequacy of the vetting process and the ability to ensure accountability.

3. Insufficient focus on drug addiction prevention and treatment:

Critics argue that U.S. military training programs have predominantly focused on law enforcement and military capabilities, neglecting the equally important aspect of drug addiction prevention and treatment. This limited focus may not address the root causes of drug trafficking and may undermine efforts to reduce demand.

4. Inadequate support for economic development:

While financial aid has been provided for alternative livelihoods and economic development in regions affected by drug trafficking and insurgent groups, critics argue that the support has been insufficient. The lack of sustained economic opportunities in these regions can contribute to the perpetuation of illegal activities.

Conclusion:

Despite the challenges and criticisms surrounding U.S. military training programs, it is important to acknowledge their role in supporting Colombian efforts to combat drug trafficking and insurgent groups. However, a critical evaluation of these programs is necessary to ensure their continued efficacy. Addressing concerns such as limited effectiveness, human rights issues, the need for drug addiction prevention and treatment, and adequate economic support will be crucial for future success. The collaboration between diplomats, historians, and policymakers is essential in shaping future military assistance programs to effectively address these challenges and criticisms.

Chapter 3: Financial Aid for Colombian Counter-Narcotics Operations

U.S. financial assistance for Colombian counter-narcotics efforts

The United States has played a significant role in supporting Colombian counter-narcotics efforts, providing both financial aid and military assistance. This subchapter explores the various ways in which the U.S. has contributed to combating drug trafficking and insurgent groups in Colombia.

Financial aid has been crucial in enabling Colombian law enforcement agencies to effectively intercept drugs and dismantle the networks involved in drug trafficking. The U.S. has provided substantial funding to enhance the capabilities of Colombian agencies involved in drug interdiction. This support has facilitated the purchase of advanced equipment, training programs, and intelligence sharing, enabling Colombian forces to carry out successful operations against drug cartels.

Moreover, U.S. financial assistance has also been directed towards programs aimed at drug addiction prevention and treatment. Recognizing the importance of addressing the root causes of drug abuse, the U.S. has invested in Colombian initiatives focused on education, rehabilitation, and social integration. These programs have been instrumental in reducing drug addiction rates and providing support to affected communities.

In addition to financial aid, the U.S. military has been actively involved in training programs for the Colombian armed forces. These programs have aimed to enhance the capabilities of Colombian troops in countering insurgent groups and drug traffickers. Through joint exercises and knowledge transfer, the U.S. has helped strengthen

Colombia's military capacity, enabling them to effectively combat the threats posed by insurgent groups and drug cartels.

Furthermore, the U.S. has provided intelligence gathering and surveillance assistance to Colombian forces. This support has been critical in identifying and tracking the movements of drug traffickers and insurgent groups. By sharing vital information and employing advanced surveillance technology, the U.S. has significantly contributed to improving the Colombian government's understanding of the dynamics of drug trafficking and insurgency.

U.S. financial assistance has also targeted the disruption of money laundering networks related to drug trafficking. By supporting Colombian efforts in this area, the U.S. has helped disrupt the financial infrastructure that sustains drug cartels. This has made it increasingly difficult for these criminal organizations to operate, further diminishing their ability to carry out illicit activities.

Additionally, the U.S. has invested in Colombian programs focused on alternative livelihoods and economic development in regions affected by drug trafficking and insurgent groups. By promoting sustainable economic opportunities, the U.S. aims to provide viable alternatives to communities previously dependent on the drug trade. This approach not only supports the long-term stability of these regions but also undermines the influence of insurgent groups and drug cartels.

In conclusion, U.S. financial assistance and military support have played a vital role in Colombia's efforts to combat drug trafficking and insurgent groups. By investing in law enforcement agencies, intelligence gathering, alternative livelihood programs, and military training, the U.S. has significantly contributed to the progress made by Colombia in countering these threats. The partnership between the two countries continues to be crucial in ensuring the security and stability of Colombia and the wider region.

Allocation and distribution of funds

In the battle against drug trafficking and insurgent groups in Colombia, the allocation and distribution of funds play a crucial role in the success of the efforts. The United States, as an ally and supporter of Colombia, has been actively involved in providing financial aid and military assistance to combat these challenges. This subchapter aims to shed light on the various aspects of allocation and distribution of funds in this context.

One of the primary areas where funds are allocated is the U.S. military's role in combating drug trafficking and insurgent groups in Colombia. The United States has provided substantial financial aid to support Colombian counter-narcotics operations. This aid is used to enhance law enforcement agencies' capabilities in drug interdiction, intelligence gathering, and surveillance. The funds are crucial for training programs for the Colombian armed forces, equipping them with the necessary skills and resources to combat these threats effectively.

In addition to military support, financial assistance is also channeled towards Colombian programs aimed at drug addiction prevention and treatment. Recognizing the importance of addressing the root causes of drug trafficking, the United States provides funds for programs that focus on alternative livelihoods and economic development in regions affected by drug trafficking and insurgent groups. These initiatives aim to provide opportunities for individuals to break free from the cycle of drug dependency and find sustainable sources of income.

Furthermore, the United States provides financial aid to support Colombian efforts in border security and drug trafficking prevention. This assistance is crucial in strengthening border controls and disrupting money laundering networks related to drug trafficking. By focusing on dismantling and neutralizing drug cartels, the funds contribute to undermining the financial backbone of these criminal organizations.

It is essential to mention that the allocation and distribution of funds are conducted with careful consideration and in close coordination with Colombian authorities. The collaboration between the United States and Colombia is built on mutual trust and a shared objective of combating drug trafficking and insurgent groups. Diplomats and historians studying this topic will find valuable insights into the intricate process of allocating funds and the impact it has on the ground.

In conclusion, the allocation and distribution of funds play a vital role in the fight against drug trafficking and insurgent groups in Colombia. The United States' financial aid and military assistance support various aspects, including training programs, intelligence gathering, interdiction operations, and programs focused on addiction prevention and alternative livelihoods. The careful allocation of funds ensures effective utilization and contributes to the overall success of the efforts. Diplomats and historians will find this subchapter informative in understanding the intricate dynamics of U.S. military and financial aid to Colombia in combating these challenges.

Programs and initiatives supported by U.S. financial aid

Programs and initiatives supported by U.S. financial aid have played a crucial role in the battle against drug trafficking and insurgent groups in Colombia. This chapter highlights the various ways in which the United States has provided assistance to Colombia, focusing on the military and financial aspects.

One of the key areas of support has been the U.S. military training programs for the Colombian armed forces. These programs have helped enhance the capabilities of the Colombian military in their fight against drug trafficking and insurgent groups. Through training in counterinsurgency tactics, intelligence gathering, and strategic planning, the Colombian armed forces have been able to better confront the challenges they face.

Financial aid has also been instrumental in supporting Colombian counter-narcotics operations. The United States has provided funding for the purchase of equipment, such as helicopters and surveillance technology, which have significantly enhanced Colombia's ability to detect and interdict drug shipments. Additionally, financial assistance has been allocated to Colombian law enforcement agencies to strengthen their capacity in drug interdiction and border security.

In addition to combating drug trafficking, the U.S. military has provided support to Colombian efforts in combating insurgent groups. This assistance includes intelligence gathering and surveillance, which have been essential in identifying and neutralizing insurgent activities. Moreover, U.S. military aid has been crucial in dismantling and neutralizing drug cartels, which often collaborate with these insurgent groups.

Financial aid has also been directed towards programs aimed at drug addiction prevention and treatment. Recognizing the importance of addressing the root causes of drug trafficking, the United States has supported Colombian initiatives to prevent drug addiction and provide treatment for those affected by it.

Furthermore, U.S. financial aid has been allocated to support Colombian efforts in border security and drug trafficking prevention. This includes assistance in improving border infrastructure, developing effective surveillance systems, and training border patrol agents.

Efforts to disrupt money laundering networks related to drug trafficking have also received significant financial assistance from the

United States. This aid has been crucial in identifying and dismantling the financial structures that support the drug trade.

Lastly, the United States has provided financial aid for Colombian programs focused on alternative livelihoods and economic development in regions affected by drug trafficking and insurgent groups. These programs aim to provide viable alternatives for communities that have long relied on illicit activities.

In conclusion, the programs and initiatives supported by U.S. financial aid have played a crucial role in Colombia's battle against drug trafficking and insurgent groups. The combination of military support and financial assistance has enhanced the capabilities of Colombian security forces, disrupted criminal networks, and contributed to long-term solutions in affected regions. The partnership between the United States and Colombia continues to be a vital component in addressing these challenges and promoting stability in the region.

Effectiveness of U.S. financial aid in combating drug trafficking

Subchapter Title: Effectiveness of U.S. Financial Aid in Combating Drug Trafficking

Introduction:

The Battle for Colombia: U.S. Military's Role in Combating Drug Trafficking and Insurgent Groups explores the extensive efforts of the United States to assist Colombia in its fight against drug trafficking and insurgent groups. This subchapter examines the effectiveness of U.S. financial aid in combating drug trafficking, highlighting its impact on various aspects of Colombian society and the ongoing struggle to eradicate this illicit trade.

U.S. Military and Financial Aid to Colombia to Combat Drug Trafficking and Insurgent Groups:

The United States has provided significant financial aid to Colombia as part of its overall strategy to combat drug trafficking and insurgent groups. This aid has been instrumental in strengthening Colombian law enforcement agencies, supporting military training programs, and enhancing intelligence gathering and surveillance capabilities.

Financial Aid for Colombian Counter-Narcotics Operations:

U.S. financial assistance has enabled Colombia to intensify its counter-narcotics operations, leading to increased drug seizures and the dismantling of major drug trafficking networks. Through the provision of resources and equipment, the U.S. has empowered Colombian forces to disrupt the production, transportation, and distribution of illicit drugs.

U.S. Military Support for Colombian Efforts to Combat Insurgent Groups:

In addition to countering drug trafficking, U.S. financial aid has bolstered Colombian efforts to combat insurgent groups. By enhancing the capabilities of the Colombian armed forces and supporting intelligence sharing, the U.S. has contributed to the successful neutralization of key leaders and the degradation of insurgent networks.

Financial Assistance for Colombian Law Enforcement Agencies in Drug Interdiction:

U.S. financial aid has played a crucial role in enhancing the capabilities of Colombian law enforcement agencies in drug interdiction. Increased funding has facilitated the development of specialized units, the provision of advanced technology, and the training of personnel, resulting in more effective drug interdiction efforts.

Conclusion:

The effectiveness of U.S. financial aid in combating drug trafficking in Colombia cannot be understated. Through its support for counter-narcotics operations, military training programs, intelligence gathering, and law enforcement efforts, the United States has significantly contributed to the fight against drug trafficking and insurgent groups. However, the battle is far from over, and continued financial aid is crucial to sustaining and further strengthening Colombian efforts to eradicate drug trafficking and bring stability to the region.

Future prospects and challenges in financial aid for counter-narcotics operations

As the battle against drug trafficking and insurgent groups in Colombia continues, it becomes crucial to assess the future prospects and challenges in providing financial aid to support these efforts. This subchapter aims to shed light on the evolving landscape of financial assistance and its implications for the U.S. military's role in combating these threats.

Looking ahead, one of the key prospects lies in strengthening the coordination and effectiveness of financial aid programs. Diplomats and historians recognize the necessity of aligning financial support with specific objectives, such as intelligence gathering, surveillance, and border security. This strategic approach ensures that resources are utilized optimally to disrupt drug trafficking networks and neutralize cartels.

However, challenges persist in this endeavor. One major challenge is the ever-changing nature of drug trafficking and insurgent groups. As these groups adapt their tactics and strategies, financial aid programs must also evolve to keep pace. This requires continuous evaluation and adaptation of the approaches employed by the U.S. military and financial aid providers.

Another challenge lies in the need for sustainable solutions. Financial aid should not solely focus on short-term gains but also prioritize long-term stability and development. This necessitates investing in programs aimed at drug addiction prevention, treatment, and alternative livelihoods. By addressing the root causes of drug trafficking and insurgency, financial aid can contribute to the overall stability of Colombia in the future.

Moreover, the subchapter explores the importance of financial aid in disrupting money laundering networks associated with drug trafficking. Efforts to dismantle these networks require robust financial assistance, as well as close collaboration between U.S. military forces and Colombian law enforcement agencies. The subchapter delves into the challenges faced in identifying and dismantling these networks and the potential for financial aid to enhance these efforts.

In conclusion, the future prospects of financial aid for counter-narcotics operations in Colombia are promising yet challenging. Diplomats and historians, along with the niches of U.S. military and financial aid to Colombia, recognize the need for coordinated efforts and sustainable solutions. By addressing these challenges head-on, financial aid can play a vital role in supporting Colombian efforts to combat drug trafficking and insurgent groups, ultimately contributing to a more stable and secure Colombia.

Chapter 4: U.S. Military Support for Colombian Efforts to Combat Insurgent Groups

U.S. military's role in supporting Colombian efforts against insurgent groups

The U.S. military has played a crucial role in supporting Colombian efforts against insurgent groups, as detailed in the subchapter titled "U.S. military's role in supporting Colombian efforts against insurgent groups" from the book "The Battle for Colombia: U.S. Military's Role in Combating Drug Trafficking and Insurgent Groups." This subchapter is addressed to an audience of diplomats and historians, as well as individuals interested in the niches of U.S. military and financial aid to Colombia, counter-narcotics operations, and the fight against insurgent groups.

Throughout the years, the U.S. has provided significant financial aid to Colombia to combat drug trafficking and insurgent groups. This aid has been crucial in supporting Colombian armed forces through military training programs. These programs have helped enhance the capabilities and effectiveness of the Colombian armed forces in their fight against insurgent groups.

In addition to military training, the U.S. has also provided financial assistance for Colombian counter-narcotics operations. This aid has been utilized to strengthen law enforcement agencies in their efforts to intercept and seize narcotics shipments. The U.S. military has also provided support for intelligence gathering and surveillance in Colombia, enabling Colombian authorities to better track and disrupt drug trafficking networks.

Furthermore, the U.S. has provided financial aid for Colombian programs aimed at drug addiction prevention and treatment. These programs have focused on addressing the root causes of drug addiction and providing support to individuals affected by drug abuse.

The U.S. military has also supported Colombian efforts in border security and drug trafficking prevention. This assistance has helped strengthen border control measures and enhance the capacity of Colombian authorities to intercept drug shipments before they reach international markets.

Additionally, financial assistance has been provided to Colombia to disrupt money laundering networks associated with drug trafficking. By targeting these networks, Colombian authorities have been able to undermine the financial infrastructure of drug cartels, making it more difficult for them to operate.

Lastly, the U.S. has supported Colombian programs focused on alternative livelihoods and economic development in regions affected by drug trafficking and insurgent groups. By providing economic opportunities and promoting sustainable development, these programs aim to address the underlying causes of insurgency and drug trafficking.

In conclusion, the U.S. military has played a vital role in supporting Colombian efforts against insurgent groups. Through financial aid, military training programs, support for counter-narcotics operations, intelligence gathering, and surveillance, the U.S. has helped enhance Colombia's capabilities in combating drug trafficking and insurgent groups. Additionally, financial assistance has been provided for drug addiction prevention and treatment, border security, disruption of money laundering networks, and economic development in affected regions. The collaboration between the U.S. military and Colombia has been instrumental in the fight against drug trafficking and insurgent groups, contributing to the overall stability and security of the region.

Types of support provided by the U.S. military

In the battle against drug trafficking and insurgent groups in Colombia, the U.S. military has played a significant role by providing various types of support. This chapter aims to shed light on the different forms of assistance extended by the U.S. military in their collaboration with Colombia, addressing the interests of diplomats and historians.

One crucial aspect of the U.S. military's involvement is financial aid. The United States has allocated substantial resources to support Colombian counter-narcotics operations. This financial assistance aims to bolster the Colombian armed forces, law enforcement agencies, and intelligence gathering and surveillance capabilities.

To enhance the Colombian armed forces' effectiveness, the U.S. military has implemented training programs. These programs focus on equipping Colombian troops with the necessary skills and knowledge to combat insurgent groups and drug cartels effectively. Through collaborative training initiatives, the U.S. military aims to strengthen the Colombian armed forces' capabilities and improve their operational effectiveness.

In addition to financial aid and training, the U.S. military also provides support for intelligence gathering and surveillance efforts in Colombia. By sharing their expertise and advanced technologies, the U.S. military aids Colombian authorities in monitoring and tracking drug trafficking activities and insurgent groups' movements. This support enables more targeted and efficient operations against these illicit networks.

Furthermore, the U.S. military extends financial assistance to Colombian programs aimed at drug addiction prevention and treatment. Recognizing the importance of addressing the root causes of drug trafficking, the U.S. military supports initiatives that promote drug addiction awareness, prevention, and rehabilitation.

The U.S. military also aids Colombian efforts in border security and drug trafficking prevention. With their expertise and resources, they assist in securing Colombia's borders, preventing the entry and exit of illicit drugs, and ensuring the safety and security of its citizens.

Moreover, the U.S. military provides financial aid to disrupt money laundering networks associated with drug trafficking. By targeting the financial infrastructure of these criminal organizations, the U.S. military seeks to undermine their operations and weaken their influence.

Lastly, the U.S. military supports Colombian programs focused on alternative livelihoods and economic development in regions affected by drug trafficking and insurgent groups. By promoting economic opportunities and sustainable development, they aim to provide viable alternatives to communities previously dependent on illicit activities.

In conclusion, the U.S. military's support in Colombia encompasses a wide range of areas, addressing the challenges posed by drug trafficking and insurgent groups. Through financial aid, training programs, intelligence gathering, and various other initiatives, the U.S. military continues to play a crucial role in combating these threats and supporting Colombia's efforts towards peace and stability.

Collaboration and coordination between U.S. and Colombian forces

In the ongoing battle against drug trafficking and insurgent groups in Colombia, collaboration and coordination between the U.S. and Colombian forces have been vital. This subchapter explores the significant role played by the U.S. military in supporting Colombia's efforts and the financial aid provided to combat these threats. It also sheds light on the various programs and initiatives that have been implemented to address drug addiction prevention, border security, intelligence gathering, and economic development.

The collaboration between the U.S. and Colombian forces has been crucial in combating drug trafficking. The U.S. has provided extensive financial aid to Colombia to support counter-narcotics operations, intelligence gathering, and surveillance efforts. This has strengthened Colombia's ability to disrupt money laundering networks associated with drug trafficking and dismantle drug cartels. The U.S. military's assistance in intelligence gathering and surveillance has been instrumental in identifying and neutralizing these criminal organizations.

Additionally, the U.S. has supported Colombian law enforcement agencies in drug interdiction efforts. Financial aid has been provided to enhance their capabilities, enabling them to effectively tackle drug trafficking at various levels. This collaboration has resulted in the seizure of significant quantities of drugs and the disruption of drug smuggling routes.

Furthermore, the U.S. military has played a crucial role in supporting Colombian efforts to combat insurgent groups. This collaboration has involved providing military training programs for the Colombian armed forces, which has enhanced their skills and capabilities. The U.S. has also provided financial assistance for programs focused on alternative livelihoods and economic development in regions affected by drug trafficking and insurgent groups. These initiatives aim to address the root causes of insurgency and offer viable alternatives to individuals involved in these activities.

The collaboration and coordination between U.S. and Colombian forces have not only strengthened Colombia's ability to combat drug trafficking and insurgent groups but also fostered a strong bilateral relationship. The partnership has evolved over the years, with both countries working together towards a common goal of achieving peace and stability in Colombia.

In conclusion, the collaboration and coordination between U.S. and Colombian forces have been instrumental in the battle against drug trafficking and insurgent groups. The financial aid provided by the U.S. has supported various programs and initiatives aimed at tackling these threats. The partnership between the two countries has not only strengthened Colombia's capacity but also fostered a strong relationship based on shared interests and objectives.

Impact of U.S. military support on Colombian counter-insurgency operations

The Impact of U.S. Military Support on Colombian Counter-Insurgency Operations

In the complex battle against drug trafficking and insurgent groups in Colombia, the support of the United States military has played a crucial role. This subchapter explores the impact of U.S. military assistance on Colombian counter-insurgency operations, highlighting its significance in combating these interconnected challenges.

One of the key aspects of U.S. military support has been the provision of financial aid to Colombia to combat drug trafficking and insurgent groups. This financial assistance has enabled the Colombian armed forces to enhance their capabilities, acquire modern equipment, and improve their operational effectiveness. Through this aid, the United States has helped strengthen Colombia's ability to disrupt drug trafficking networks and combat insurgent groups, thereby contributing to regional stability.

The U.S. military has also been instrumental in providing training programs to the Colombian armed forces. These programs have focused on improving their tactical skills, intelligence gathering, and surveillance capabilities. By sharing their expertise and knowledge, U.S. trainers have helped Colombian forces become more effective in their counter-insurgency operations.

Financial aid has not only supported Colombian counter-narcotics operations but has also augmented the efforts of law enforcement agencies in drug interdiction. The United States has provided resources to enhance Colombia's ability to disrupt money laundering networks associated with drug trafficking. By targeting the financial infrastructure of drug cartels, this support has weakened their operations and hindered their ability to sustain themselves.

Furthermore, U.S. military assistance has facilitated intelligence gathering and surveillance efforts in Colombia. By sharing advanced technology and providing logistical support, the United States has helped Colombian forces collect vital information on drug trafficking and insurgent activities. This intelligence has been crucial in identifying targets, planning operations, and neutralizing threats.

In addition to these direct interventions, U.S. financial aid has supported Colombian programs aimed at drug addiction prevention and treatment. By investing in these initiatives, the United States has contributed to breaking the cycle of drug addiction, reducing the demand for illicit drugs, and creating healthier communities.

U.S. military aid has also been pivotal in supporting Colombian efforts in border security and drug trafficking prevention. By providing resources for border surveillance, training, and infrastructure development, the United States has helped Colombia strengthen its borders, preventing the entry and exit of illicit drugs and insurgent groups.

Moreover, financial assistance has played a crucial role in supporting Colombian programs focused on alternative livelihoods and economic development in regions affected by drug trafficking and insurgent groups. By promoting sustainable economic opportunities, these initiatives have provided viable alternatives to communities previously dependent on illicit activities, thereby undermining the influence of drug cartels and insurgent groups.

In conclusion, the impact of U.S. military support on Colombian counter-insurgency operations has been significant. Through financial aid, training programs, intelligence sharing, and support for various initiatives, the United States has played a vital role in strengthening Colombia's ability to combat drug trafficking and insurgent groups. This support has not only contributed to regional stability but has also fostered economic development and promoted the well-being of Colombian communities affected by these challenges.

Criticisms and controversies surrounding U.S. military involvement in fighting insurgent groups

The battle against drug trafficking and insurgent groups in Colombia has long been a topic of debate and controversy. As the United States has played a significant role in supporting Colombian efforts through military aid, financial assistance, and training programs, it is essential to examine the criticisms surrounding this involvement.

One of the primary criticisms revolves around the potential negative consequences of U.S. military support for Colombian armed forces. Critics argue that such assistance may inadvertently contribute to human rights abuses, as some Colombian units have been accused of targeting civilians and engaging in extrajudicial killings. Diplomats and historians have raised concerns about the lack of accountability and oversight in these operations, urging the U.S. government to ensure that its aid does not exacerbate the existing human rights challenges in Colombia.

Moreover, financial aid for Colombian counter-narcotics operations has faced criticism for its limited effectiveness in reducing drug production and trafficking. Despite significant investments, drug cartels continue to thrive, and drug-related violence remains a grave concern. Critics argue that a more comprehensive approach, focusing on social and economic development, is necessary to address the root causes of drug trafficking and insurgency.

Additionally, the U.S. military support for Colombian efforts to combat insurgent groups has raised questions about the alignment of interests. Some argue that the U.S. government's focus on counter-terrorism has overshadowed the need for a comprehensive peace process, potentially hindering long-term stability in the region. Diplomats and historians stress the importance of addressing the underlying socio-economic factors that fuel insurgency, rather than relying solely on military intervention.

Furthermore, concerns have been raised about the allocation of financial assistance. While significant funds have been dedicated to law enforcement agencies and military operations, critics argue that more resources should be directed towards drug addiction prevention, treatment, and alternative livelihood programs. This approach would not only address the demand for drugs but also provide viable alternatives to communities affected by drug trafficking and insurgency.

In conclusion, the U.S. military's role in combating drug trafficking and insurgent groups in Colombia has faced criticisms and controversies. Diplomats and historians highlight the need for careful oversight, accountability, and a comprehensive approach that addresses the root causes of the problem. By considering these concerns, the United States can refine its strategies and ensure that its involvement supports long-term peace, stability, and development in Colombia.

Chapter 5: Financial Assistance for Colombian Law Enforcement Agencies in Drug Interdiction

U.S. financial aid for Colombian law enforcement agencies

The United States has played a crucial role in supporting Colombian law enforcement agencies in their fight against drug trafficking and insurgent groups. Through financial aid, the U.S. government has provided substantial resources to strengthen Colombia's ability to combat these threats and promote stability in the region.

One of the primary objectives of U.S. financial aid has been to enhance Colombian law enforcement agencies' capacity to intercept and interdict illegal drug shipments. With the assistance of U.S. funding, Colombian authorities have been able to acquire advanced technology, such as radar systems and surveillance equipment, to improve their capabilities in detecting and tracking drug traffickers' movements.

Furthermore, the U.S. has provided financial assistance for programs aimed at preventing drug addiction and supporting drug treatment and rehabilitation efforts. Recognizing the underlying socioeconomic factors that contribute to drug abuse, the U.S. has supported initiatives in Colombia that focus on alternative livelihoods and economic development in regions affected by drug trafficking and insurgent groups. By promoting sustainable economic opportunities, these programs aim to reduce the reliance on illicit activities and provide a path towards stability and prosperity.

In addition to supporting counter-narcotics operations, the U.S. has also aided Colombian law enforcement agencies in intelligence gathering and surveillance activities. Through financial aid, the U.S. has facilitated the training and equipping of Colombian intelligence units, enabling them to effectively collect and analyze information critical to combating drug trafficking networks and insurgent groups.

Moreover, U.S. financial aid has supported Colombian efforts to disrupt money laundering networks associated with drug trafficking. By providing resources for financial investigations and strengthening anti-money laundering measures, the U.S. has helped Colombia to dismantle the financial infrastructure that sustains drug cartels and insurgent groups.

The U.S. has also been a key partner in enhancing Colombian border security and preventing drug trafficking across international boundaries. Financial assistance has enabled Colombia to invest in border surveillance technology, infrastructure, and training to detect and deter illicit activities along its borders.

Through a comprehensive approach that combines financial aid with military support, the United States has demonstrated its commitment to Colombia's security and stability. By empowering Colombian law enforcement agencies, the U.S. has contributed significantly to the country's progress in combating drug trafficking and insurgent groups. The positive impact of U.S. financial aid can be seen in the improved capabilities and effectiveness of Colombian law enforcement agencies, as well as the reduction in drug-related violence and instability in the country.

For diplomats and historians studying the U.S. military's role in combating drug trafficking and insurgent groups, understanding the extent and impact of U.S. financial aid for Colombian law enforcement agencies is crucial. This subchapter sheds light on the various areas in which the U.S. has provided financial assistance and highlights the significant progress achieved through this partnership. It serves as a valuable resource for anyone interested in the complex dynamics of

U.S. military and financial aid to Colombia and its impact on promoting security and stability in the region.

Funding allocation and utilization for drug interdiction efforts

In the ongoing battle against drug trafficking and insurgent groups in Colombia, funding allocation and utilization play a crucial role. This subchapter aims to shed light on the various aspects of financial aid and military support provided by the United States to Colombia in their fight against these challenges.

The United States, recognizing the severity of the drug trafficking problem in Colombia, has been a key partner in providing financial assistance to combat this issue. Through various programs, the U.S. allocates funds to support Colombian counter-narcotics operations, intelligence gathering, and surveillance. These funds enable Colombian law enforcement agencies to enhance their capacity for drug interdiction and disrupt money laundering networks associated with drug trafficking.

The U.S. military also plays a significant role in supporting Colombian efforts to combat insurgent groups. Military aid is provided to train and equip the Colombian armed forces, enabling them to effectively counter these groups. Additionally, the U.S. provides assistance in border security and drug trafficking prevention, ensuring that Colombian efforts to disrupt drug cartels are successful.

Financial aid is not limited to military support alone. The United States recognizes the importance of addressing the root causes of drug trafficking and insurgency in Colombia. Therefore, funds are allocated to programs aimed at drug addiction prevention and treatment, as well as alternative livelihoods and economic development in regions affected by drug trafficking and insurgent groups. By offering support in these areas, the U.S. aims to create lasting solutions and opportunities for affected communities.

The allocation and utilization of funding for drug interdiction efforts have been carefully planned and implemented to maximize their impact. Diplomats and historians studying the U.S. Military's role in combating drug trafficking and insurgent groups in Colombia will find this subchapter invaluable in understanding the financial aid and military support provided by the United States. It highlights the comprehensive approach taken to address the multifaceted challenges posed by drug trafficking and insurgency and offers insights into the effectiveness of these efforts.

Overall, the United States' funding allocation and utilization for drug interdiction efforts in Colombia reflect a commitment to supporting the country's fight against drug trafficking and insurgent groups. Through financial aid and military support, the U.S. aims to strengthen Colombian institutions, empower local communities, and ultimately create a safer and more prosperous Colombia.

Collaborative initiatives between U.S. and Colombian law enforcement

Collaborative initiatives between U.S. and Colombian law enforcement have played a crucial role in combating drug trafficking and insurgent groups in Colombia. These initiatives, marked by both military and financial aid, have been instrumental in strengthening the capacity of Colombian law enforcement agencies and fostering effective cooperation between the two nations.

One of the key areas of collaboration has been the provision of U.S. military training programs for the Colombian armed forces. These programs have enhanced the professionalism and operational capabilities of Colombian military units engaged in counter-narcotics and counterinsurgency operations. Through joint exercises and training sessions, U.S. personnel have shared their expertise and knowledge in areas such as intelligence gathering, surveillance, and border security, thereby enabling their Colombian counterparts to better identify and combat drug trafficking networks and insurgent groups.

Financial aid has also played a pivotal role in supporting Colombian counter-narcotics operations. The U.S. government has provided substantial funding to Colombian law enforcement agencies involved in drug interdiction efforts. This financial assistance has helped in the procurement of advanced equipment, such as helicopters and surveillance technologies, which are vital in conducting successful operations against drug cartels.

Furthermore, U.S. military assistance has been crucial in intelligence gathering and surveillance in Colombia. Through the sharing of information and intelligence, Colombian law enforcement agencies have been able to improve their understanding of the strategies and tactics employed by drug cartels and insurgent groups. This collaboration has led to more effective operations, resulting in the dismantling and neutralization of major drug cartels operating within Colombia.

Financial aid has also been directed towards Colombian programs aimed at drug addiction prevention and treatment. Recognizing the importance of addressing the root causes of drug trafficking, the U.S. has provided financial support to initiatives focusing on education, awareness, and rehabilitation. By investing in these programs, the U.S. aims to reduce drug demand and provide alternative paths for individuals trapped in the cycle of addiction.

Additionally, U.S. military aid has supported Colombian efforts in border security and drug trafficking prevention. This assistance has included the provision of equipment and training to strengthen border control measures and enhance interagency coordination in combating drug trafficking along Colombia's borders.

Financial assistance has also been directed towards disrupting money laundering networks related to drug trafficking. By targeting the financial infrastructure of drug cartels, these initiatives aim to undermine their operations and hinder their ability to profit from illicit activities.

Lastly, financial aid has supported Colombian programs focused on alternative livelihoods and economic development in regions affected by drug trafficking and insurgent groups. Through investment in infrastructure, agriculture, and entrepreneurship, these programs seek to provide local communities with sustainable alternatives to the drug trade, thereby reducing their vulnerability to the influence of insurgent groups.

In conclusion, collaborative initiatives between U.S. and Colombian law enforcement have been vital in the battle against drug trafficking and insurgent groups in Colombia. Through the provision of military and financial aid, the U.S. has contributed to the strengthening of Colombian law enforcement agencies, intelligence gathering capabilities, border security, and the disruption of drug cartels. Furthermore, financial support has been directed towards drug addiction prevention, alternative livelihoods, and economic development, all of which are critical in creating a sustainable and secure future for Colombia.

Successes and challenges in financial aid for drug interdiction

Financial aid has played a crucial role in supporting Colombia's efforts to combat drug trafficking and insurgent groups. Over the years, the United States has been a key partner in providing both military assistance and financial support to address these pressing issues. This subchapter explores the successes and challenges encountered in the financial aid provided for drug interdiction in Colombia.

One of the significant successes in financial aid for drug interdiction has been the support provided to Colombian law enforcement agencies. The financial assistance has enabled these agencies to enhance their capabilities in terms of equipment, training, and intelligence gathering. As a result, there has been a notable increase in drug seizures and the dismantling of drug trafficking networks. This success has not only improved Colombia's security situation but has also contributed to the disruption of money laundering networks associated with drug trafficking.

Another area of success has been the financial aid directed towards alternative livelihoods and economic development in regions affected by drug trafficking and insurgent groups. By providing resources and support for sustainable economic projects, the aid has helped create opportunities for individuals to move away from the drug trade and gain legitimate income. This has not only reduced the influence of drug cartels but also contributed to the overall development of these regions.

However, financial aid for drug interdiction in Colombia has also faced significant challenges. One of the primary challenges has been ensuring the effective utilization of the funds provided. It is crucial to have proper oversight and accountability mechanisms in place to prevent misuse or corruption. Additionally, coordinating the efforts of multiple stakeholders, including Colombian law enforcement agencies, the military, and international partners, can be complex and requires ongoing coordination and communication.

Another challenge has been the long-term sustainability of the programs supported by financial aid. While immediate successes can be achieved, it is essential to ensure that the progress made is maintained over the long term. This necessitates continued financial support and a comprehensive approach that addresses not only the symptoms but also the root causes of the drug trade and insurgent groups.

In conclusion, financial aid has played a critical role in Colombia's efforts to combat drug trafficking and insurgent groups. The successes achieved include improved law enforcement capabilities, increased drug seizures, disrupted money laundering networks, and the promotion of alternative livelihoods. However, challenges remain, including ensuring effective utilization of funds and long-term sustainability. By addressing these challenges, financial aid can continue to be an essential tool in the battle against drug trafficking and insurgent groups in Colombia.

Future prospects for financial assistance in enhancing law enforcement capabilities

As the battle against drug trafficking and insurgent groups in Colombia continues, the prospects for financial assistance in enhancing law enforcement capabilities are promising. The United States military has played a crucial role in supporting Colombian efforts through various programs and aid initiatives. Looking ahead, there are several key areas where future assistance can significantly contribute to the ongoing fight against these challenges.

Financial aid for Colombian law enforcement agencies in drug interdiction remains a critical aspect of combating drug trafficking. Enhanced funding can support the procurement of advanced equipment and technology, such as surveillance systems, communication devices, and forensic laboratories. This assistance will bolster the effectiveness and efficiency of law enforcement agencies in intercepting drug shipments and dismantling criminal networks.

Furthermore, financial assistance can be directed towards intelligence gathering and surveillance in Colombia. The United States military has already provided significant support in this area, but continued investment is necessary to enhance capabilities further. Funding can be allocated to training programs for intelligence officers, the establishment of intelligence fusion centers, and the development of advanced data analysis tools. These efforts will enable law enforcement agencies to anticipate and respond to emerging threats more effectively.

In addition to intelligence and drug interdiction, financial aid can also be utilized to disrupt money laundering networks related to drug trafficking. By targeting the financial infrastructure of criminal organizations, law enforcement agencies can severely hamper their operations. Enhanced funding will facilitate the establishment of specialized units dedicated to investigating and dismantling these networks, leading to significant disruptions in their illicit activities.

Moreover, future prospects for financial assistance lie in supporting Colombian programs focused on alternative livelihoods and economic development in regions affected by drug trafficking and insurgent groups. By offering viable alternatives to communities involved in the drug trade, the cycle of violence and dependency can be broken. Investments in education, job creation, and infrastructure projects will empower these communities and reduce their vulnerability to recruitment by insurgent groups or involvement in drug-related activities.

In conclusion, the future prospects for financial assistance in enhancing law enforcement capabilities in Colombia are promising. Diplomats and historians recognize the importance of continued support from the United States military in various areas such as drug interdiction, intelligence gathering, money laundering disruption, and community development. By investing in these critical areas, we can contribute to a safer and more prosperous Colombia while combating drug trafficking and insurgent groups effectively.

Chapter 6: U.S. Military Assistance for Intelligence Gathering and Surveillance in Colombia

Role of U.S. military in intelligence gathering and surveillance operations

The Battle for Colombia: U.S. Military's Role in Combating Drug Trafficking and Insurgent Groups

In the ongoing battle against drug trafficking and insurgent groups in Colombia, the role of the U.S. military in intelligence gathering and surveillance operations has been crucial. This subchapter aims to provide insights into the extent of U.S. military involvement in these areas, highlighting its impact on the overall efforts to combat these threats.

Intelligence gathering is a fundamental component of any successful counter-narcotics and counter-insurgency strategy. The U.S. military has played a pivotal role in assisting Colombian forces in collecting and analyzing vital intelligence that has helped identify key drug trafficking routes, dismantle drug cartels, and neutralize insurgent groups. Through the use of advanced surveillance technologies, including drones and satellite imagery, the U.S. military has provided the Colombian armed forces with invaluable information, enabling them to target drug traffickers and insurgents with precision.

Furthermore, the U.S. military has conducted extensive training programs for Colombian armed forces, equipping them with the necessary skills and knowledge to effectively carry out intelligence gathering and surveillance operations. These programs have not only enhanced the capabilities of the Colombian military but have also fostered closer cooperation and coordination between the two nations in combating drug trafficking and insurgent groups.

Financial aid has been another crucial aspect of U.S. support in intelligence gathering and surveillance operations. The United States has provided substantial financial assistance to Colombia, enabling the implementation of programs aimed at improving the capacity of Colombian law enforcement agencies in drug interdiction. These funds have been utilized to acquire state-of-the-art surveillance equipment, enhance communication infrastructure, and train personnel in intelligence analysis.

Moreover, U.S. military aid has extended beyond intelligence gathering and surveillance to include support for Colombian efforts in border security and drug trafficking prevention. The U.S. military has provided resources and training to strengthen Colombia's ability to protect its borders from drug traffickers and other criminal elements. This assistance has been vital in preventing the infiltration of drugs and weapons into Colombian territory.

In conclusion, the role of the U.S. military in intelligence gathering and surveillance operations in Colombia has been pivotal in the battle against drug trafficking and insurgent groups. Through extensive training programs, financial aid, and the provision of advanced surveillance technologies, the U.S. military has significantly enhanced the capacity of Colombian forces in collecting actionable intelligence. This collaboration has not only led to the dismantling of drug cartels and neutralization of insurgent groups but has also strengthened bilateral ties between the U.S. and Colombia in their shared commitment to combating these threats.

Technological support and equipment provided by the U.S.

The United States has played a crucial role in supporting Colombia's efforts to combat drug trafficking and insurgent groups through the provision of advanced technological support and equipment. This subchapter delves into the various ways in which the U.S. has assisted Colombia in enhancing its capabilities to tackle these pressing challenges.

One of the key areas where the U.S. has provided technological support is in intelligence gathering and surveillance. Through its advanced satellite systems and cutting-edge reconnaissance aircraft, the U.S. has aided Colombian forces in tracking and monitoring the movements of drug traffickers and insurgent groups. This has been instrumental in identifying key targets and disrupting their operations.

Furthermore, the U.S. has supplied Colombia with state-of-the-art equipment for border security and drug trafficking prevention. This includes the provision of radar systems, night vision devices, and thermal imaging cameras, which have significantly bolstered Colombia's ability to detect and intercept illicit drug shipments. Such support has been vital in curbing the flow of narcotics and preventing them from reaching international markets.

In addition, the U.S. has contributed to Colombian law enforcement agencies' efforts in drug interdiction through financial aid. This funding has enabled the purchase of specialized equipment such as drug-sniffing dogs, body scanners, and advanced drug testing kits. These tools have proven invaluable in identifying and apprehending individuals involved in narcotics trafficking, as well as detecting hidden drug caches.

Moreover, the U.S. has extended its technological support to Colombian programs focused on alternative livelihoods and economic development in regions affected by drug trafficking and insurgent groups. Through the provision of computer systems, software, and training, the U.S. has helped local communities to diversify their economies and reduce their dependence on illicit activities. This has not only created new opportunities but also contributed to long-term stability and security.

The U.S. has also assisted Colombian efforts to disrupt money laundering networks related to drug trafficking. By providing advanced financial tracking software and expertise, the U.S. has aided Colombian authorities in identifying and dismantling these illicit networks. This has not only disrupted the flow of funds to drug cartels but also helped in prosecuting individuals involved in money laundering.

In conclusion, the U.S. has been a crucial partner in providing technological support and equipment to Colombia in its battle against drug trafficking and insurgent groups. Through advanced surveillance systems, border security equipment, financial tracking software, and other cutting-edge tools, the U.S. has significantly enhanced Colombia's capabilities. This assistance has not only helped in combating these pressing challenges but has also contributed to the overall security and stability of the region.

Collaboration between U.S. and Colombian intelligence agencies

The battle against drug trafficking and insurgent groups in Colombia has been a matter of international concern for many years. Recognizing the need for a coordinated effort to combat these threats, the intelligence agencies of the United States and Colombia have formed a strong partnership. This collaboration has proven to be instrumental in the success of various initiatives aimed at tackling drug trafficking and insurgency in Colombia.

The collaboration between U.S. and Colombian intelligence agencies has been multifaceted, encompassing intelligence sharing, joint training programs, and the provision of financial aid. Through the exchange of vital intelligence information, these agencies have managed to stay one step ahead of drug traffickers and insurgent groups, effectively disrupting their operations and dismantling their networks.

Furthermore, the U.S. has played a crucial role in providing training programs for the Colombian armed forces. This training has not only enhanced the capabilities of the Colombian military but has also fostered a spirit of cooperation and collaboration between the two countries. By equipping Colombian forces with the necessary skills and knowledge, the U.S. has empowered them to effectively combat drug trafficking and insurgent groups within their borders.

Financial aid has also played a significant role in the fight against drug trafficking and insurgency in Colombia. The U.S. has provided substantial financial assistance for a range of counter-narcotics operations, law enforcement agencies, and programs aimed at drug addiction prevention and treatment. Additionally, financial aid has been instrumental in supporting efforts to disrupt money laundering networks related to drug trafficking and in promoting alternative livelihoods and economic development in regions affected by these illicit activities.

In addition to intelligence sharing and financial assistance, the U.S. has provided significant military support to Colombian efforts in border security and drug trafficking prevention. This support has included the provision of equipment, technology, and expertise to enhance surveillance and intelligence gathering capabilities. By strengthening border security and preventing the flow of drugs, the U.S. and Colombian intelligence agencies have made significant strides in mitigating the impact of drug trafficking and insurgency in the region.

The collaboration between U.S. and Colombian intelligence agencies has been a vital component in the battle against drug trafficking and insurgency in Colombia. Through intelligence sharing, joint training programs, and financial aid, these agencies have worked together to disrupt the operations of drug traffickers and insurgent groups, strengthen law enforcement capabilities, and promote alternative livelihoods. This partnership stands as a testament to the power of international collaboration in addressing complex security challenges.

Impact of U.S. military assistance on intelligence capabilities

Title: Impact of U.S. Military Assistance on Intelligence Capabilities in Colombia

Introduction:

The United States' military assistance has played a pivotal role in strengthening Colombia's intelligence capabilities in combating drug trafficking and insurgent groups. This subchapter explores the significant impact of U.S. military support on intelligence gathering, surveillance, and related operations in Colombia. Aimed at diplomats and historians, this section sheds light on the various dimensions of U.S.-Colombia collaboration and its effectiveness in combating these pressing challenges.

Enhancing Intelligence Capabilities:

One of the key contributions of U.S. military assistance to Colombia has been the provision of advanced intelligence equipment and technology. By supplying state-of-the-art surveillance systems, satellite imagery, and communication tools, the U.S. has significantly bolstered Colombia's ability to gather critical information on drug trafficking networks and insurgent activities. This support has enabled Colombian law enforcement agencies to monitor and disrupt criminal networks with greater precision, ultimately leading to increased interdiction rates and the dismantling of drug cartels.

Intelligence Sharing and Collaboration:

The U.S. military has also played a pivotal role in intelligence sharing and collaboration with Colombian counterparts. Through joint training programs and exchange of expertise, American intelligence agencies have helped enhance the capabilities of Colombian intelligence units. This collaboration has not only improved information sharing between the two countries but has also fostered greater regional cooperation in combating transnational criminal organizations.

Support for Counter-Narcotics Operations:

Financial aid provided by the U.S. has been instrumental in supporting Colombian counter-narcotics operations. These funds have been utilized to develop sophisticated intelligence networks, strengthen human intelligence capabilities, and enhance interagency coordination. By investing in these areas, the U.S. has helped Colombia disrupt money laundering networks, target drug cartels, and interdict drug shipments more effectively.

Border Security and Regional Cooperation:

U.S. military aid has also focused on supporting Colombian efforts to enhance border security and prevent drug trafficking. By providing training and resources, the U.S. has supported the Colombian armed forces in securing their borders, thereby preventing the flow of drugs and weapons. This assistance has not only improved regional stability but has also strengthened cooperation between Colombia and its neighboring countries in combating drug trafficking.

Conclusion:

The U.S. military assistance has had a transformative impact on Colombia's intelligence capabilities, empowering the country to combat drug trafficking and insurgent groups more effectively. Through intelligence sharing, advanced technology, financial aid, and collaborative training programs, the U.S. has helped Colombia dismantle drug cartels, disrupt criminal networks, and strengthen border security. This support has not only contributed to regional stability but has also paved the way for long-term economic development and the promotion of alternative livelihoods in drug-affected regions. The partnership between the U.S. military and Colombia serves as a testament to the importance of international cooperation in addressing complex security challenges.

Ethical and legal considerations in intelligence cooperation

Intelligence cooperation between nations plays a crucial role in combating drug trafficking and insurgent groups. However, this collaboration raises several ethical and legal considerations that must be addressed. This subchapter aims to explore these concerns and shed light on the complex issues faced by diplomats and historians in the context of U.S. military's role in Colombia.

From an ethical standpoint, intelligence cooperation must uphold principles of transparency, accountability, and respect for human rights. Diplomats and historians need to examine the moral implications of sharing intelligence with Colombia, considering the country's history of human rights abuses and corruption. This requires careful evaluation of the Colombian armed forces' adherence to international norms and standards.

Furthermore, legal considerations come into play when sharing sensitive information. Diplomats and historians must navigate the boundaries of national laws and international agreements to ensure that intelligence cooperation does not violate privacy rights or undermine judicial processes. The subchapter will explore the legal frameworks governing intelligence sharing and the challenges faced in striking a balance between security imperatives and individual rights.

Within the niches of U.S. military and financial aid to Colombia, intelligence cooperation raises specific ethical and legal concerns. The subchapter will delve into the complexities of U.S. military training programs for Colombian armed forces and the need to ensure that training does not contribute to human rights violations. It will also discuss the legal obligations of financial aid for counter-narcotics operations and the importance of preventing funds from being misused or going into the wrong hands.

In the realm of intelligence gathering and surveillance, diplomats and historians must grapple with questions of privacy, consent, and the potential for abuse. The subchapter will explore the ethical implications of U.S. military assistance in intelligence operations and the legal frameworks in place to protect individuals' rights.

Additionally, financial assistance for Colombian law enforcement agencies and efforts to disrupt money laundering networks must be examined from both ethical and legal perspectives. The subchapter will delve into the challenges of balancing the need for effective law enforcement with the risk of corrupt practices and abuse of power.

In conclusion, the subchapter "Ethical and Legal Considerations in Intelligence Cooperation" will provide diplomats and historians with a comprehensive analysis of the complex ethical and legal landscape surrounding intelligence cooperation in Colombia. By addressing these concerns, it aims to foster a more informed and nuanced understanding of the U.S. military's role in combating drug trafficking and insurgent groups, ultimately contributing to more effective and responsible interventions in the future.

Chapter 7: Financial Aid for Colombian Programs Aimed at Drug Addiction Prevention and Treatment

U.S. financial aid for Colombian drug addiction prevention programs

In the battle against drug trafficking and insurgent groups in Colombia, the United States has played a significant role not only in providing military support but also in offering financial aid for various programs aimed at combating the drug epidemic. One crucial aspect of this assistance lies in the funding provided for Colombian drug addiction prevention programs.

Recognizing that tackling drug addiction is just as vital as targeting drug traffickers, the U.S. government has allocated substantial resources to support Colombia's efforts in this area. Diplomats and historians have closely followed the U.S. financial aid initiatives, understanding the importance of addressing drug addiction as a root cause of the drug trade.

Through financial assistance, the United States has aided Colombian law enforcement agencies in establishing comprehensive drug interdiction strategies. These initiatives focus not only on disrupting drug trafficking networks but also on preventing drug addiction through education, awareness campaigns, and treatment programs. By investing in prevention, the U.S. aims to reduce the demand for illicit drugs and thereby weaken the influence and power of drug cartels.

Additionally, financial aid has been crucial in supporting Colombian programs directed at drug addiction prevention and treatment. These programs not only target individuals struggling with addiction but also focus on vulnerable populations, such as youth and marginalized communities. By providing resources for counseling, rehabilitation, and community support, the U.S. aims to mitigate the social and economic impact of drug addiction.

In conjunction with financial aid, the U.S. military has also played a role in supporting Colombian efforts by providing intelligence gathering and surveillance capabilities. This support enables law enforcement agencies to identify drug trafficking routes, apprehend traffickers, and disrupt money laundering networks associated with drug trafficking.

Furthermore, financial assistance has been instrumental in implementing alternative livelihood programs and promoting economic development in regions affected by drug trafficking and insurgent groups. By investing in sustainable economic opportunities, the U.S. aims to reduce the allure of the drug trade and provide viable alternatives for communities formerly dependent on illicit activities.

Overall, the U.S. financial aid for Colombian drug addiction prevention programs serves as a crucial component in the broader battle against drug trafficking and insurgent groups. By addressing the root causes of the drug trade, the United States aims to create a safer and more stable Colombia, benefiting not only the Colombian people but also regional and global security. The continued support and collaboration between the U.S. and Colombia in this endeavor are essential for long-term success.

Funding allocation and utilization for prevention and treatment initiatives

In the ongoing battle against drug trafficking and insurgent groups in Colombia, the allocation and utilization of funding play a crucial role in the success of prevention and treatment initiatives. This subchapter aims to shed light on how the United States military has been instrumental in providing financial aid and support to Colombia in combating these pressing issues.

The United States has been a key partner in providing financial assistance to Colombia's counter-narcotics operations. Through various programs, the U.S. has allocated significant funds to support Colombian law enforcement agencies in drug interdiction efforts. This assistance has facilitated the training of Colombian armed forces in counter-narcotics operations, enabling them to effectively combat drug trafficking networks.

Furthermore, the United States has extended its support to Colombian efforts in combating insurgent groups. Financial aid has been directed towards intelligence gathering and surveillance activities, enabling Colombian security forces to gather critical information on these groups' movements and activities. This assistance has not only bolstered Colombia's security apparatus but has also facilitated cooperation and coordination between the two nations.

Recognizing the importance of drug addiction prevention and treatment, the United States has also provided financial aid for Colombian programs in this area. These initiatives focus on not only preventing drug addiction but also providing treatment and rehabilitation for those affected. By addressing the root causes of drug addiction, these programs contribute to the long-term stability and security of Colombia.

In addition to these efforts, the United States has supported Colombian endeavors in border security and preventing drug trafficking. Financial aid and military assistance have been provided to strengthen border security measures, ensuring that drug trafficking routes are disrupted and intercepted. This assistance also extends to efforts aimed at dismantling and neutralizing drug cartels, which pose a significant threat to Colombia's stability.

Recognizing the socio-economic impact of drug trafficking and insurgent groups, the United States has also allocated funds to support alternative livelihoods and economic development in regions affected by these issues. By providing opportunities for economic growth and stability, these programs seek to address the root causes of drug trafficking and insurgency.

In conclusion, the United States military's role in combating drug trafficking and insurgent groups in Colombia extends beyond military training and support. The allocation and utilization of funding for prevention and treatment initiatives have been crucial in addressing the underlying causes of these issues. Through financial aid and support, the United States has contributed significantly to Colombia's efforts, working hand in hand towards a safer and more secure future.

Collaborative efforts in addressing drug addiction in Colombia

Drug addiction is a pressing issue in Colombia, with devastating consequences for individuals, communities, and the nation as a whole. To effectively combat this problem, collaborative efforts between the United States and Colombia have been essential. This subchapter explores the various ways in which these collaborative efforts have been instrumental in addressing drug addiction in Colombia.

One key aspect of this collaboration is the financial aid provided by the United States to Colombia for programs aimed at drug addiction prevention and treatment. Through this financial assistance, Colombia has been able to establish and enhance rehabilitation centers, expand access to quality healthcare, and develop comprehensive prevention campaigns. These efforts have helped raise awareness about the dangers of drug addiction and promote a culture of drug-free living.

In addition to financial aid, the United States has also provided extensive support through its military assistance programs. This

programs that have proven effective in regions affected by drug trafficking and insurgent groups.

In conclusion, supporting drug addiction programs in the context of combating drug trafficking and insurgent groups in Colombia poses various challenges. However, by addressing resource allocation, societal barriers, coordination, research, and international cooperation, diplomats and historians can contribute to the development of effective programs that not only address drug addiction but also contribute to long-term stability and security in Colombia.

Chapter 8: U.S. Military Aid to Support Colombian Efforts in Border Security and Drug Trafficking Prevention

U.S. military's role in supporting Colombian border security efforts

The United States military has played a significant role in supporting Colombian border security efforts as part of its broader mission to combat drug trafficking and insurgent groups. This subchapter explores the various ways in which the U.S. military has provided assistance to Colombia in order to enhance its border security and prevent the illicit flow of drugs across its borders.

One crucial aspect of U.S. support has been through financial aid. The United States has allocated substantial funds to Colombia to combat drug trafficking and insurgent groups, with a focus on border security. This financial aid has enabled Colombia to strengthen its border control infrastructure, enhance surveillance capabilities, and invest in advanced technologies to detect and interdict drug shipments.

In addition to financial assistance, the U.S. military has also provided training programs for the Colombian armed forces. These programs have aimed to enhance the capabilities of Colombian troops in conducting border patrols, intelligence gathering, and interdiction operations. Through these training programs, Colombian forces have been able to develop the necessary skills and expertise to effectively secure the country's borders.

Moreover, the U.S. military has supported Colombian efforts to combat insurgent groups that pose a threat to border security. By providing intelligence gathering and surveillance capabilities, the U.S. military has helped Colombian forces in identifying and neutralizing insurgent networks operating near the borders. This support has

significantly contributed to reducing the influence of these groups and enhancing overall border security.

Financial aid has also been channeled towards Colombian law enforcement agencies involved in drug interdiction. This assistance has enabled these agencies to enhance their capacity to disrupt drug trafficking networks, confiscate illicit drugs, and prosecute individuals involved in drug-related activities.

Furthermore, the U.S. military has provided assistance for intelligence gathering and surveillance in Colombia. Through the deployment of advanced technologies and equipment, the U.S. military has helped Colombian forces in monitoring and tracking drug trafficking activities along the borders. This support has been instrumental in identifying key routes used by drug traffickers and intercepting their shipments.

Financial aid has also been crucial in supporting Colombian programs aimed at drug addiction prevention and treatment. These programs have focused on providing education, counseling, and rehabilitation services to individuals affected by drug addiction, thereby addressing the root causes of drug trafficking and reducing demand.

In conclusion, the U.S. military has played a vital role in supporting Colombian border security efforts. Through financial aid, training programs, intelligence gathering, and surveillance assistance, the U.S. has helped Colombia enhance its capabilities in combating drug trafficking and insurgent groups. This support has not only contributed to improving border security but has also helped Colombia disrupt money laundering networks, dismantle drug cartels, and promote alternative livelihoods in regions affected by drug trafficking and insurgent groups.

Joint operations and cooperation between U.S. and Colombian forces

Joint operations and cooperation between U.S. and Colombian forces have played a crucial role in combating drug trafficking and insurgent groups in Colombia. This subchapter explores the close collaboration between these two nations, highlighting the significant impact it has had on the country's security landscape.

The partnership between the U.S. and Colombian forces has been a cornerstone in the fight against drug trafficking. Through financial aid, the U.S. has provided substantial resources to support Colombian counter-narcotics operations. This assistance has enabled the Colombian armed forces to enhance their capabilities and effectively target drug production and trafficking networks.

Furthermore, the U.S. has been instrumental in providing military training programs for the Colombian armed forces. These programs have focused on equipping Colombian personnel with the necessary skills and knowledge to combat drug trafficking and insurgent groups effectively. The collaboration in intelligence gathering and surveillance has also been crucial in identifying and neutralizing high-value targets within these criminal organizations.

Financial aid has not only been directed towards military efforts but has also supported Colombian law enforcement agencies in drug interdiction. This assistance has bolstered the capacity of Colombian authorities to intercept drugs, seize assets, and disrupt money laundering networks associated with drug trafficking.

The U.S. military has also extended support to Colombian efforts in combating insurgent groups. Through intelligence sharing and joint operations, both nations have effectively targeted and dismantled these organizations, significantly reducing their influence and operational capabilities.

Recognizing the multifaceted nature of the drug problem, financial aid has been directed towards programs aimed at drug addiction prevention and treatment in Colombia. This holistic approach acknowledges the importance of addressing the root causes of drug abuse and supporting affected communities.

The partnership between the U.S. and Colombian forces extends beyond the fight against drug trafficking. U.S. military aid has also supported Colombian efforts in border security and drug trafficking prevention. By enhancing border surveillance and interdiction capabilities, both nations have effectively curtailed the flow of drugs across their shared borders.

Additionally, financial assistance has been directed towards programs focused on alternative livelihoods and economic development in regions affected by drug trafficking and insurgent groups. These initiatives aim to provide sustainable alternatives to drug cultivation and offer opportunities for economic growth and stability.

The joint operations and cooperation between U.S. and Colombian forces have been pivotal in combating drug trafficking and insurgent groups in Colombia. This collaboration has not only strengthened the security landscape but has also contributed to the overall stability and development of the nation. The close ties between these two nations serve as a model for successful international partnerships in addressing complex security challenges.

Equipment and technology provided by the U.S. for border security

The United States has played a crucial role in supporting Colombia's efforts to combat drug trafficking and insurgent groups. As part of this collaboration, the U.S. has provided significant equipment and technology to enhance Colombia's border security measures. This subchapter will delve into the various contributions made by the U.S.

in terms of equipment and technology in the ongoing battle for Colombia.

One of the key areas where the U.S. has provided assistance is in the field of intelligence gathering and surveillance. The U.S. military has shared advanced surveillance technology, including unmanned aerial vehicles (UAVs) and radar systems, to help monitor Colombia's borders more effectively. These tools have proven instrumental in detecting and intercepting drug trafficking activities, as well as identifying and neutralizing insurgent groups operating along the border regions.

In addition to surveillance technology, the U.S. has also supplied Colombia with cutting-edge communication equipment. This has greatly improved the coordination and response capabilities of Colombian law enforcement agencies, as well as the armed forces. Enhanced communication systems have facilitated real-time information sharing, enabling more efficient and targeted operations against drug cartels and insurgent groups. With the help of the U.S., Colombian security forces are better equipped to respond swiftly to emerging threats and prevent drug trafficking across their borders.

Furthermore, the U.S. has provided training and equipment to bolster Colombia's border interdiction efforts. This includes providing specialized equipment such as night vision goggles, thermal imaging devices, and detection systems to enhance the abilities of Colombian security forces in identifying and intercepting drug shipments. The U.S. has also supported Colombia with canine units trained in drug detection to further strengthen border security.

The provision of equipment and technology by the U.S. has not been limited to border control measures alone. It has extended to supporting Colombian efforts in disrupting money laundering networks related to drug trafficking. Advanced financial tracking technology and expertise have been shared, enabling Colombian authorities to trace and seize

illicit funds associated with drug cartels. By targeting the financial infrastructure of drug trafficking organizations, Colombia has been able to deal a significant blow to their operations.

In conclusion, the U.S. has been instrumental in equipping Colombia with the necessary technology and equipment to strengthen its border security measures. The collaboration has enhanced intelligence gathering, surveillance capabilities, communication systems, interdiction efforts, and financial tracking. These contributions have significantly bolstered Colombia's ability to combat drug trafficking and insurgent groups, ultimately leading to a safer and more secure nation.

Effectiveness of U.S. military aid in preventing drug trafficking

The United States has long been involved in providing military aid to Colombia to combat drug trafficking and insurgent groups. This subchapter explores the effectiveness of this aid in achieving its intended goals and its impact on various aspects of Colombian society.

U.S. military aid to Colombia to combat drug trafficking and insurgent groups has been a key component of the country's efforts to address these challenges. The provision of financial assistance, military training programs, and intelligence gathering and surveillance support has significantly enhanced Colombia's ability to disrupt drug trafficking networks and neutralize insurgent groups.

One of the most notable impacts of U.S. military aid has been the support provided to Colombian law enforcement agencies in drug interdiction. Through training programs and financial assistance, the U.S. has helped strengthen the capabilities of Colombian forces in intercepting drug shipments and apprehending key individuals involved in the trade. This has directly contributed to a decline in the availability of illegal drugs in the U.S. market, thereby reducing the profitability of drug trafficking.

Furthermore, U.S. military aid has played a crucial role in supporting Colombian efforts to combat insurgent groups, such as the Revolutionary Armed Forces of Colombia (FARC) and the National Liberation Army (ELN). By providing intelligence, logistical support, and training, the U.S. has enabled Colombian forces to weaken these groups and disrupt their operations. This has not only enhanced the security situation in Colombia but also contributed to regional stability.

In addition to direct military assistance, the U.S. has also provided financial aid for Colombian programs aimed at drug addiction prevention and treatment. This investment in public health initiatives has helped reduce drug demand within Colombia, addressing the root causes of the drug trade.

Moreover, U.S. military aid has supported Colombian efforts in border security and drug trafficking prevention. By providing resources for enhanced surveillance and infrastructure along the Colombian borders, the U.S. has helped prevent the illicit flow of drugs across international boundaries.

Lastly, the U.S. has supported Colombian programs focused on alternative livelihoods and economic development in regions affected by drug trafficking and insurgent groups. By promoting sustainable economic opportunities, the aim is to provide alternatives to communities that have traditionally relied on the drug trade for their livelihoods. This approach not only reduces the attractiveness of engaging in drug trafficking but also contributes to long-term stability and development in Colombia.

In conclusion, U.S. military aid has been instrumental in preventing drug trafficking and combating insurgent groups in Colombia. Through financial assistance, training programs, intelligence support, and a focus on public health and economic development, the U.S. has made significant contributions to the overall efforts of the Colombian government. However, ongoing challenges remain, and it is important for diplomats and historians to continuously evaluate the effectiveness of this aid and explore ways to further enhance its impact.

Future challenges and opportunities in border security collaboration

As the battle against drug trafficking and insurgent groups in Colombia continues, it is crucial for the United States military and other key stakeholders to address the future challenges and opportunities in border security collaboration. The effectiveness of border security measures directly impacts the success of efforts to combat drug trafficking and insurgent activities, making it a pressing issue for diplomats and historians to understand and work towards.

One of the major challenges in border security collaboration is the vast and rugged terrain that spans the Colombia border. The diverse landscapes, including dense jungles, mountain ranges, and rivers, provide hiding places and transit routes for drug traffickers and insurgent groups. As a result, it is essential for the U.S. military to enhance its surveillance capabilities, intelligence gathering, and training programs for the Colombian armed forces. This collaboration will enable the development of effective strategies to detect and intercept illicit activities along the border.

Moreover, the financial aid provided to Colombia for counter-narcotics operations should be channeled towards strengthening law enforcement agencies involved in drug interdiction. This includes investing in advanced technology and equipment, such as radar systems and drones, to enhance surveillance capabilities.

Additionally, financial assistance should be allocated to programs aimed at drug addiction prevention and treatment, as reducing drug demand is crucial in combating the drug trade.

Another significant challenge is the disruption of money laundering networks associated with drug trafficking. Financial aid should be directed towards supporting Colombian efforts to disrupt these networks and dismantle drug cartels. This can be achieved through training programs and intelligence sharing to identify and target key individuals and organizations involved in money laundering.

In terms of opportunities, collaboration between the U.S. military and Colombian authorities presents a chance to strengthen border security and prevent drug trafficking. Joint operations, intelligence sharing, and the exchange of best practices can enhance the effectiveness of border control efforts. Furthermore, financial aid can be utilized to support programs focused on alternative livelihoods and economic development in regions affected by drug trafficking and insurgent groups. By providing opportunities for local communities, the risk of individuals becoming involved in illicit activities can be reduced.

In conclusion, future challenges and opportunities in border security collaboration are crucial areas of focus for diplomats and historians studying the U.S. military's role in combating drug trafficking and insurgent groups in Colombia. By addressing these challenges and seizing opportunities, the fight against drug trafficking and insurgency can be strengthened, leading to a safer and more stable Colombia.

Chapter 9: Financial Assistance for Colombian Efforts to Disrupt Money Laundering Networks Related to Drug Trafficking

U.S. financial aid for Colombian anti-money laundering initiatives

In the ongoing battle against drug trafficking and insurgent groups in Colombia, the United States has played a crucial role in providing financial aid to support various initiatives aimed at combating these issues. One such area where U.S. assistance has been instrumental is in Colombian anti-money laundering efforts.

Money laundering is a significant challenge in the fight against drug trafficking and insurgent groups, as it allows criminals to legitimize their illicit proceeds and continue their illegal activities. Recognizing the importance of disrupting these networks, the U.S. has provided substantial financial aid to Colombia to strengthen its anti-money laundering capabilities.

Through targeted assistance programs, the U.S. has supported Colombian law enforcement agencies in their efforts to disrupt money laundering networks related to drug trafficking. This assistance has included funding for training and capacity building, as well as the provision of advanced technology and equipment for intelligence gathering and surveillance.

Furthermore, U.S. financial aid has been directed towards programs focused on alternative livelihoods and economic development in regions affected by drug trafficking and insurgent groups. By investing in these initiatives, the U.S. aims to address the root causes of drug production and create sustainable economic opportunities for affected communities, thereby reducing their vulnerability to criminal activities.

In addition to financial aid, the U.S. military has also provided support for Colombian efforts to dismantle and neutralize drug cartels. This assistance has included training programs for the Colombian armed forces, aimed at enhancing their capabilities in counter-narcotics operations. By strengthening the Colombian military's capacity to combat drug trafficking, the U.S. hopes to disrupt the activities of insurgent groups who rely on the drug trade for funding.

The U.S. recognizes that a comprehensive approach is necessary to effectively combat drug trafficking and insurgent groups in Colombia. Therefore, financial aid for Colombian anti-money laundering initiatives is just one component of a broader strategy that includes military support, intelligence gathering, border security, and drug addiction prevention and treatment.

In conclusion, U.S. financial aid for Colombian anti-money laundering initiatives plays a critical role in the overall efforts to combat drug trafficking and insurgent groups in the country. By disrupting money laundering networks, supporting alternative livelihoods, and strengthening law enforcement capabilities, the U.S. aims to undermine the financial foundations of criminal organizations and create a more secure and prosperous future for Colombia.

Allocation and utilization of funds for disrupting money laundering networks

In the ongoing battle against drug trafficking and insurgent groups in Colombia, the allocation and utilization of funds play a critical role. As diplomats and historians delve into the intricate dynamics of this conflict, it becomes evident that disrupting money laundering networks is a key component in dismantling the infrastructure that supports these illicit activities.

The United States, recognizing the urgency and gravity of the situation, has been at the forefront of providing financial aid to Colombia. This aid serves multiple purposes, including supporting Colombian law enforcement agencies in their efforts to interdict drugs and combat money laundering. By allocating funds specifically for disrupting money laundering networks, the U.S. ensures that the fight against drug trafficking and insurgent groups is tackled comprehensively.

The financial assistance provided by the U.S. is channeled into various programs aimed at disrupting money laundering networks. One critical aspect is intelligence gathering and surveillance, where the U.S. military plays a pivotal role. Through the provision of military assistance, Colombia can enhance its intelligence capabilities, enabling the identification and neutralization of key individuals and organizations involved in money laundering.

Moreover, financial aid supports Colombian programs focused on drug addiction prevention and treatment. By addressing the root causes of drug addiction, Colombia aims to reduce the demand for illicit drugs, consequently disrupting the profitability of money laundering networks. These programs not only save lives but also contribute to the overall objective of dismantling the infrastructure that supports drug trafficking.

Another area where financial aid is crucial is in supporting Colombian efforts to disrupt money laundering networks related to drug trafficking. By allocating funds for these operations, the U.S. military aids in the dismantling and neutralization of drug cartels. This targeted approach seeks to disrupt the financial networks that sustain their operations, making it harder for them to operate and expand their influence.

Furthermore, financial assistance is channeled into Colombian programs focused on alternative livelihoods and economic development in regions affected by drug trafficking and insurgent groups. By investing in these regions, the aim is to provide viable alternatives to individuals involved in illicit activities, ultimately disrupting the cycle of drug trafficking and insurgency.

In conclusion, the allocation and utilization of funds for disrupting money laundering networks are of utmost importance in the battle against drug trafficking and insurgent groups in Colombia. Through financial aid, the U.S. military supports Colombian efforts in intelligence gathering, surveillance, and dismantling drug cartels. Additionally, funds are allocated for programs focused on drug addiction prevention, alternative livelihoods, and economic development. By disrupting the financial networks that sustain these illicit activities, Colombia moves closer to achieving lasting peace and stability.

Collaborative efforts between U.S. and Colombian agencies in combating money laundering

Money laundering has long been a significant issue in Colombia, with drug trafficking organizations using sophisticated methods to hide and legitimize their illicit profits. Recognizing the need for a coordinated response, the United States and Colombian agencies have joined forces to combat this menace. Through close collaboration, these two nations have made significant strides in disrupting money laundering networks related to drug trafficking.

The partnership between U.S. and Colombian agencies is built on a strong foundation of trust and shared objectives. Diplomats and historians studying this collaboration will find a wealth of information on the joint efforts to combat money laundering in Colombia within the context of the broader battle against drug trafficking and insurgent groups.

U.S. financial aid plays a crucial role in supporting Colombian counter-narcotics operations. This assistance provides the necessary resources to enhance the capabilities of Colombian law enforcement agencies in drug interdiction. Moreover, financial aid is directed towards intelligence gathering and surveillance efforts, allowing for a more effective response to drug trafficking activities.

The U.S. military has also been instrumental in supporting Colombian efforts to combat insurgent groups. By providing training programs for the Colombian armed forces, the U.S. has helped strengthen their capabilities in border security and drug trafficking prevention. Additionally, financial assistance is directed towards programs aimed at drug addiction prevention and treatment, addressing the root causes of drug trafficking.

One of the key focus areas of collaborative efforts between U.S. and Colombian agencies is disrupting money laundering networks. Financial aid is allocated to Colombian programs that aim to dismantle and neutralize drug cartels. By targeting the financial infrastructure of these organizations, the U.S. and Colombian agencies have successfully disrupted their operations.

Furthermore, financial assistance is also directed towards programs focused on alternative livelihoods and economic development in regions affected by drug trafficking and insurgent groups. By providing opportunities for legal employment and economic growth, these programs offer individuals an alternative to engaging in illicit activities.

The collaborative efforts between U.S. and Colombian agencies in combating money laundering exemplify the strong partnership between the two nations. Diplomats and historians studying this topic will find valuable insights into the multifaceted approach employed to disrupt money laundering networks related to drug trafficking. This subchapter sheds light on the pivotal role played by U.S. military and financial aid in supporting Colombian efforts to combat drug trafficking and insurgent groups, ultimately contributing to a more secure and prosperous Colombia.

Impact of U.S. financial assistance on disrupting money laundering networks

Money laundering is a critical component of the global drug trade, enabling criminal organizations to legitimize their illicit proceeds and perpetuate their criminal activities. As the United States plays a crucial role in combating drug trafficking and insurgent groups in Colombia, its financial assistance has had a significant impact on disrupting money laundering networks in the country.

The U.S. government has been actively providing financial aid to Colombian law enforcement agencies involved in drug interdiction operations. This assistance has not only strengthened the capabilities of Colombian authorities to detect and seize drug-related assets but has also facilitated intelligence gathering and surveillance efforts. By providing resources for advanced technology and training programs, the U.S. has enabled Colombian law enforcement agencies to effectively target money laundering networks.

Furthermore, U.S. financial aid has supported Colombian programs aimed at drug addiction prevention and treatment. By addressing the root causes of drug abuse, these programs play a vital role in reducing the demand for illicit drugs and, consequently, the profitability of money laundering networks. By focusing on prevention and treatment, the U.S. aid has disrupted the economic incentives that drive money laundering activities.

In addition to law enforcement and drug addiction programs, U.S. financial assistance has also supported Colombian efforts in border security and drug trafficking prevention. By strengthening border control measures and enhancing the capacity of Colombian armed forces, the U.S. aid has made it more difficult for criminal organizations to transport illicit drugs and launder their proceeds across borders.

Moreover, the U.S. has provided financial aid for Colombian programs focused on alternative livelihoods and economic development in regions affected by drug trafficking and insurgent groups. By creating sustainable economic opportunities for local communities, the U.S. aid has reduced the vulnerability of these regions to money laundering networks. It has empowered individuals to pursue legitimate means of income, thereby diminishing the attractiveness of engaging in criminal activities.

In conclusion, the impact of U.S. financial assistance on disrupting money laundering networks in Colombia cannot be overstated. Through its support for law enforcement agencies, drug addiction prevention programs, border security efforts, and economic development initiatives, the U.S. has made significant strides in dismantling the financial infrastructure of drug cartels and insurgent groups. By targeting the economic aspects of the drug trade, the U.S. aid has disrupted money laundering networks and contributed to a more secure and prosperous Colombia.

Future strategies and challenges in targeting money laundering associated with drug trafficking

As the battle against drug trafficking and insurgent groups in Colombia intensifies, it is crucial for diplomats and historians to understand the future strategies and challenges in targeting money laundering associated with this illicit trade. Money laundering plays a pivotal role in sustaining drug trafficking networks, enabling them to maintain their operations and evade law enforcement efforts. In order to effectively combat this issue, the U.S. military and financial aid to Colombia must focus on several key areas.

Firstly, there is a need for enhanced intelligence gathering and surveillance capabilities. By providing advanced technology and training to Colombian law enforcement agencies, the U.S. military can assist in identifying and tracking money laundering networks. This includes the use of sophisticated surveillance systems, data analysis tools, and cooperation with international financial institutions to trace illicit financial transactions.

Furthermore, financial aid should be directed towards Colombian programs aimed at disrupting money laundering networks. This can be achieved through partnerships with financial institutions, training for law enforcement agencies in financial investigations, and the establishment of specialized units dedicated to targeting money laundering associated with drug trafficking. By dismantling these networks, the flow of funds to drug cartels can be disrupted, severely impacting their operational capabilities.

However, it is important to acknowledge the challenges that lie ahead. The ever-evolving nature of money laundering techniques requires constant adaptation and innovation in our strategies. Criminal organizations are increasingly utilizing digital currencies and offshore accounts to conceal their illicit proceeds. To address this, the U.S. military should invest in research and development of cutting-edge technologies and expertise in financial investigations.

Additionally, the collaboration between Colombian and U.S. authorities must be strengthened. Jointly developed training programs, information sharing mechanisms, and coordinated operations are crucial for effectively targeting money laundering networks. Diplomatic efforts should focus on fostering strong bilateral relationships, enabling the exchange of ideas and best practices in combating money laundering associated with drug trafficking.

In conclusion, the future strategies and challenges in targeting money laundering associated with drug trafficking require a comprehensive approach. By focusing on intelligence gathering, disrupting money laundering networks, and fostering collaboration between Colombian and U.S. authorities, significant strides can be made in dismantling the financial infrastructure that supports drug trafficking. It is only through these concerted efforts that a lasting impact can be achieved in the battle against drug trafficking and insurgent groups in Colombia.

Chapter 10: U.S. Military Assistance for Colombian Efforts to Dismantle and Neutralize Drug Cartels

U.S. military's role in supporting Colombian operations against drug cartels

The U.S. military has played a crucial role in supporting Colombian operations against drug cartels, as detailed in the subchapter, "U.S. military's role in supporting Colombian operations against drug cartels," in the book "The Battle for Colombia: U.S. Military's Role in Combating Drug Trafficking and Insurgent Groups." This subchapter is specifically targeted towards a sophisticated audience of diplomats and historians with a vested interest in understanding the complexities of the U.S. military's involvement in Colombia.

One of the key areas where the U.S. military has provided support is through financial aid to Colombia to combat drug trafficking and insurgent groups. This assistance has been instrumental in strengthening the Colombian armed forces and enabling them to effectively combat these threats. The book explores the various ways in which this financial aid has been utilized, including the procurement of advanced military equipment and the enhancement of training programs for the Colombian armed forces.

Moreover, the U.S. military has also played a pivotal role in providing training programs to the Colombian armed forces. These programs have been designed to enhance the capabilities of Colombian military personnel in counter-narcotics operations, intelligence gathering, and surveillance. By transferring knowledge and expertise, the U.S. military has been instrumental in strengthening the Colombian armed forces' ability to effectively combat drug cartels and insurgent groups.

Financial aid has also been allocated to Colombian counter-narcotics operations, which have focused on interdicting drug shipments and disrupting money laundering networks. This support has been critical in enabling Colombian law enforcement agencies to effectively combat drug trafficking. Additionally, the U.S. military has provided support for intelligence gathering and surveillance in Colombia, facilitating the identification and neutralization of drug cartels.

Furthermore, the U.S. military has allocated financial aid to Colombian programs aimed at drug addiction prevention and treatment. Understanding the importance of addressing the root causes of drug trafficking, these programs have focused on providing alternative livelihoods and economic development in regions affected by drug trafficking and insurgent groups.

In conclusion, the U.S. military's role in supporting Colombian operations against drug cartels has been multifaceted. Through financial aid, training programs, and assistance in intelligence gathering and surveillance, the U.S. military has significantly bolstered the capabilities of Colombian armed forces and law enforcement agencies. This support has not only enabled Colombia to combat drug cartels and insurgent groups effectively but has also contributed to addressing the underlying socio-economic issues that fuel these problems. The subchapter provides a comprehensive analysis of the U.S. military's involvement, offering valuable insights for diplomats and historians interested in understanding the intricate dynamics of this partnership.

Collaboration and coordination between U.S. and Colombian forces in cartel dismantlement

One of the key aspects in the battle against drug trafficking and insurgent groups in Colombia has been the collaboration and coordination between the U.S. and Colombian forces. This partnership has played a crucial role in dismantling drug cartels and neutralizing their operations. Diplomats and historians interested in understanding the dynamics of this collaboration will find this subchapter particularly enlightening.

The U.S. has been a key ally to Colombia, providing both military and financial aid to combat drug trafficking and insurgent groups. The collaboration begins with the U.S. military training programs for the Colombian armed forces. These programs have been instrumental in enhancing the capabilities of the Colombian forces, equipping them with the necessary skills and knowledge to tackle the complex challenges posed by drug cartels and insurgent groups.

Financial aid has also played a significant role in supporting Colombian counter-narcotics operations. The U.S. has provided substantial resources to enhance the capacity of Colombian law enforcement agencies in drug interdiction. This financial assistance has been crucial in improving their capabilities to disrupt drug trafficking networks and dismantle the cartels.

Moreover, the U.S. has extended its military support to Colombian efforts in combating insurgent groups. This collaboration has involved intelligence gathering and surveillance operations, which have helped identify and neutralize key figures within these groups. The U.S. military aid has also supported Colombian efforts in border security and drug trafficking prevention, ensuring that these criminal organizations have a harder time operating in the region.

In addition to these military efforts, the U.S. has also extended financial assistance to Colombian programs aimed at drug addiction prevention and treatment. Recognizing the need for a comprehensive approach to combating drug trafficking, the U.S. has supported initiatives focused on alternative livelihoods and economic development in regions affected by drug trafficking and insurgent groups. By addressing the root causes of drug production and consumption, these programs aim to create sustainable solutions and reduce the influence of cartels.

The collaboration and coordination between U.S. and Colombian forces have been crucial in dismantling and neutralizing drug cartels operating in Colombia. This subchapter provides a comprehensive overview of the various ways in which the U.S. military has assisted Colombia in its fight against drug trafficking and insurgent groups. Diplomats and historians interested in understanding the intricacies of this partnership will find this subchapter to be an invaluable resource.

Strategies and tactics employed by U.S. military in targeting drug cartels

In the ongoing battle against drug cartels and insurgent groups in Colombia, the United States military has played a crucial role, employing a range of strategies and tactics to combat drug trafficking and promote stability in the region. This subchapter aims to provide diplomats and historians with a comprehensive understanding of the approaches taken by the U.S. military in this complex and multifaceted conflict.

One of the key strategies employed by the U.S. military has been the provision of financial aid to Colombia to combat drug trafficking and insurgent groups. This aid has been instrumental in funding various counter-narcotics operations, intelligence gathering and surveillance efforts, and programs aimed at disrupting money laundering networks associated with drug trafficking.

To effectively combat drug cartels, the U.S. military has also focused on supporting Colombian law enforcement agencies in drug interdiction. Financial assistance has been provided to enhance their capacity to detect and seize illicit drugs, dismantle trafficking networks, and prosecute key individuals involved in the drug trade.

Furthermore, the U.S. military has played a crucial role in training and providing assistance to the Colombian armed forces. This has involved equipping them with the necessary skills and resources to engage in counter-narcotics operations, border security, and drug trafficking prevention. Additionally, financial aid has been allocated to support Colombian efforts in intelligence gathering, surveillance, and dismantling and neutralizing drug cartels.

Recognizing the importance of addressing the root causes of drug trafficking and insurgency, the U.S. military has also focused on supporting Colombian programs aimed at drug addiction prevention and treatment. Financial aid has been provided to establish rehabilitation centers, promote awareness campaigns, and develop alternative livelihoods and economic development in regions affected by drug trafficking and insurgent groups.

In summary, the strategies and tactics employed by the U.S. military in targeting drug cartels in Colombia have been diverse and comprehensive. Financial aid, training programs, intelligence gathering, and surveillance efforts have all played a significant role in supporting Colombian efforts to combat drug trafficking and insurgent groups. By addressing both the supply and demand sides of the drug trade and promoting stability and development, the U.S. military has contributed to the overall success of the battle against drug cartels in Colombia.

Evaluating the impact of U.S. military assistance on cartel neutralization efforts

Introduction:

In the ongoing battle against drug trafficking and insurgent groups in Colombia, the United States has played a significant role through its military assistance programs. This subchapter aims to evaluate the impact of U.S. military assistance on cartel neutralization efforts. By analyzing the effectiveness of various initiatives, this chapter seeks to provide a comprehensive understanding of the outcomes achieved through U.S. support.

Evaluation of Military Assistance:

1. Direct Support for Counter-Narcotics Operations:

Financial aid provided by the U.S. government has enabled Colombian law enforcement agencies to enhance their drug interdiction capabilities. The assistance has facilitated the seizure of significant quantities of drugs, disrupted trafficking networks, and contributed to a reduction in drug-related violence.

2. Training and Capacity Building:

U.S. military training programs for the Colombian armed forces have strengthened their capabilities to combat insurgent groups and drug cartels effectively. The training has enhanced the professionalism, tactical skills, and strategic planning abilities of Colombian forces, leading to successful counterinsurgency and counter-narcotics operations.

3. Intelligence Gathering and Surveillance:

Through financial aid and technical support, the U.S. has assisted Colombian agencies in improving their intelligence gathering and surveillance capabilities. This collaboration has enabled the identification and neutralization of key cartel leaders, leading to significant disruptions within the drug trafficking networks.

4. Dismantling Drug Cartels:

U.S. military assistance has played a crucial role in the dismantling and neutralization of drug cartels operating in Colombia. The support has helped Colombian authorities target and capture high-value targets, disrupt money laundering networks, and seize substantial assets, thereby significantly weakening the cartels' operational capabilities.

5. Alternative Livelihoods and Economic Development:

Financial aid programs aimed at promoting alternative livelihoods and economic development in regions affected by drug trafficking and insurgent groups have had a positive impact. These initiatives create sustainable opportunities for individuals who might otherwise be drawn into illicit activities, reducing their reliance on drug cartels and insurgent groups.

Conclusion:

The evaluation of the impact of U.S. military assistance on cartel neutralization efforts in Colombia reveals significant achievements. Through financial aid, training programs, intelligence sharing, and support for alternative livelihoods, the United States has played a pivotal role in combating drug trafficking and insurgent groups. While challenges persist, the collaboration between the U.S. and Colombian authorities has resulted in notable successes, contributing to the overall security and stability of the region. Diplomats and historians studying the U.S. military's role in combating drug trafficking and insurgent groups will find this evaluation instrumental in understanding the multifaceted nature of the battle for Colombia.

Lessons learned and future prospects in dismantling drug cartels

In the battle against drug cartels, Colombia has seen significant progress over the years, thanks to the efforts and support of the U.S. military and financial aid. This subchapter aims to shed light on the lessons learned from this endeavor and explore the future prospects in dismantling drug cartels.

One of the key lessons learned is the importance of collaboration and cooperation between nations. The U.S. military's role in supporting the Colombian armed forces has proven crucial in combating drug trafficking and insurgent groups. Through training programs and intelligence sharing, both countries have been able to enhance their capabilities and effectively disrupt the operations of drug cartels.

Financial aid has played a vital role in Colombian counter-narcotics operations. The provision of resources for law enforcement agencies, intelligence gathering, and surveillance has strengthened their ability to interdict drugs and gather evidence against cartels. Additionally, financial assistance has enabled Colombian programs focused on drug addiction prevention and treatment, tackling the root causes of drug abuse.

The support provided by the U.S. military in border security and drug trafficking prevention has also been significant. By assisting in securing Colombia's borders, the flow of drugs and illegal activities has been greatly reduced. Furthermore, efforts to disrupt money laundering networks related to drug trafficking have been successful, thanks to the financial aid provided. This has severely impacted the financial capabilities of drug cartels, making it harder for them to sustain their operations.

Looking towards the future, it is essential to continue supporting Colombian efforts to dismantle and neutralize drug cartels. The lessons learned from the past have shown that a comprehensive approach, including military assistance, financial aid, and socio-economic development, is necessary to tackle the root causes of drug trafficking and insurgent groups.

Investing in alternative livelihoods and economic development in regions affected by drug trafficking and insurgent groups is crucial. By providing opportunities for the local population, we can weaken the influence of drug cartels and create a sustainable environment that discourages involvement in illicit activities.

In conclusion, the battle against drug cartels in Colombia has taught us valuable lessons. Collaboration, financial aid, and a comprehensive approach are the keys to success. By continuing to support Colombian efforts and investing in long-term solutions, we can pave the way for a future free from the clutches of drug cartels and insurgent groups.

Chapter 11: Financial Aid for Colombian Programs Focused on Alternative Livelihoods and Economic Development in Regions Affected by Drug Trafficking and Insurgent Groups

U.S. financial aid for Colombian alternative livelihood programs

In the battle against drug trafficking and insurgent groups in Colombia, the United States has played a crucial role in providing financial assistance to support various programs aimed at promoting alternative livelihoods and economic development in regions affected by these challenges. This subchapter explores the efforts and initiatives taken by the U.S. government to provide financial aid for Colombian alternative livelihood programs.

Recognizing the importance of addressing the root causes of drug trafficking and insurgency, the United States has allocated substantial funds to support Colombian programs focused on creating sustainable economic opportunities in regions heavily impacted by these issues. Through financial aid, the U.S. aims to empower local communities and reduce their reliance on illicit activities by providing them with viable alternatives.

These alternative livelihood programs encompass a wide range of initiatives, including agricultural development, vocational training, entrepreneurship support, and microfinance projects. By investing in these areas, the U.S. government aims to strengthen the economic resilience of vulnerable communities, helping them break free from the grip of drug trafficking and insurgent groups.

Moreover, the U.S. financial aid also emphasizes the importance of social inclusion and gender equality. By integrating marginalized groups, such as women and indigenous communities, into these alternative livelihood programs, the U.S. seeks to address the underlying social disparities that contribute to the perpetuation of drug trafficking and insurgency.

In addition to providing financial resources, the United States also offers technical expertise and knowledge sharing through its military training programs for the Colombian armed forces. By enhancing the capabilities of Colombian security forces in combating drug trafficking and insurgent groups, the U.S. aims to create a more stable and secure environment where alternative livelihood programs can thrive.

Overall, the U.S. financial aid for Colombian alternative livelihood programs represents a significant commitment to addressing the multifaceted challenges of drug trafficking and insurgency. By investing in sustainable economic development and inclusive social policies, the U.S. government seeks to promote long-term stability and prosperity in Colombia, while simultaneously undermining the influence of criminal organizations and insurgent groups. Through these efforts, the United States hopes to contribute to a brighter future for Colombia and its people.

Allocation and utilization of funds for economic development in affected regions

In the battle against drug trafficking and insurgent groups in Colombia, it is crucial to understand the significance of allocating and utilizing funds for economic development in the affected regions. This subchapter will delve into the importance of financial aid and military support in promoting economic growth, stability, and resilience in these areas.

The United States, recognizing the interconnectedness of economic development and security, has been at the forefront of providing financial assistance to Colombia. Diplomats and historians studying the U.S. Military and Financial Aid to Colombia to Combat Drug Trafficking and Insurgent Groups will find this subchapter particularly insightful.

One key aspect of this assistance is the provision of funds for Colombian counter-narcotics operations. The U.S. recognizes the need to support law enforcement agencies in their efforts to interdict drug shipments and disrupt money laundering networks. By allocating funds for these operations, the U.S. aids in dismantling and neutralizing drug cartels, an essential step in combating drug trafficking.

Furthermore, financial aid is directed towards Colombian programs aimed at drug addiction prevention and treatment. Recognizing that drug addiction is both a social and public health issue, the U.S. military aids in supporting these programs, which focus on prevention, treatment, and rehabilitation. By addressing the root causes of drug addiction, these programs contribute to long-term stability and reduce the demand for illicit drugs.

Economic development in affected regions is also a priority. The U.S. military aid supports Colombian efforts in border security and drug trafficking prevention, focusing on the development of comprehensive strategies to combat drug trafficking and insurgent groups effectively. Additionally, financial assistance is directed towards programs focused on alternative livelihoods and economic development in regions affected by drug trafficking and insurgent groups. By providing opportunities for sustainable economic growth, these programs aim to create stability, reduce poverty, and weaken the influence of illicit activities.

In conclusion, the allocation and utilization of funds for economic development in affected regions are crucial in the battle against drug trafficking and insurgent groups in Colombia. The U.S. military, through financial aid and support, plays a significant role in promoting economic growth, stability, and resilience. By addressing the interconnectedness of economic development and security, these efforts contribute to long-term success in combating drug trafficking and insurgent groups. Diplomats and historians will find this subchapter invaluable in understanding the multifaceted approach taken by the United States in its battle for Colombia.

Collaborative initiatives between U.S. and Colombian agencies in promoting alternative livelihoods

In the ongoing battle against drug trafficking and insurgent groups in Colombia, collaborative initiatives between U.S. and Colombian agencies have played a crucial role in promoting alternative livelihoods as a means to combat these issues. By addressing the root causes of drug trafficking and insurgency, these initiatives aim to create sustainable economic opportunities and reduce the reliance on illicit activities.

The U.S. Military and Financial Aid to Colombia to Combat Drug Trafficking and Insurgent Groups has been instrumental in providing support for various programs focused on alternative livelihoods and economic development. Through financial aid, these programs have been able to empower local communities in regions affected by drug trafficking and insurgent groups. By offering viable alternatives such as agricultural projects, vocational training, and micro-enterprise development, these initiatives have provided individuals with the means to escape the clutches of drug trafficking and insurgency.

Furthermore, U.S. military training programs for Colombian armed forces have also played a significant role in promoting alternative livelihoods. By equipping the Colombian armed forces with the necessary skills and knowledge to combat drug trafficking and insurgent groups, these training programs have enhanced their ability to protect and support local communities. This, in turn, has created a stable environment for the implementation of alternative livelihood programs.

Financial aid for Colombian programs focused on alternative livelihoods and economic development in regions affected by drug trafficking and insurgent groups has been crucial in sustaining these initiatives. By providing resources and funding, the U.S. has enabled the Colombian government to implement comprehensive strategies that address the socio-economic challenges faced by these regions. This includes investment in infrastructure, education, healthcare, and job creation, all of which are vital in providing individuals with viable alternatives to drug trafficking and insurgency.

Collaborative efforts have also extended to intelligence gathering and surveillance in Colombia. Through U.S. military assistance, Colombian agencies have been able to enhance their capabilities in gathering crucial intelligence on drug trafficking networks and insurgent groups. This intelligence has been vital in identifying areas most in need of alternative livelihood programs and targeting efforts to disrupt drug cartels and insurgency networks.

In conclusion, collaborative initiatives between U.S. and Colombian agencies have been pivotal in promoting alternative livelihoods as a means to combat drug trafficking and insurgent groups. Through financial aid, military training programs, intelligence gathering, and surveillance, these initiatives have empowered local communities and provided them with sustainable economic opportunities. By addressing the root causes of these issues, these collaborative efforts have not only contributed to the overall security and stability of Colombia but have also created a pathway towards a brighter future for its people.

U.S. Military and Financial Aid to Colombia: A Comprehensive Approach to Combating Drug Trafficking and Insurgent Groups

In the ongoing battle against drug trafficking and insurgent groups in Colombia, the United States has played a crucial role in providing both military and financial aid. This subchapter will delve into the various forms of assistance that the U.S. has extended to Colombia, highlighting the multi-faceted approach adopted to address the complex challenges faced by the country.

One of the key aspects of U.S. support has been the provision of military training programs for the Colombian armed forces. These programs aim to enhance the capabilities of the Colombian military in conducting counter-insurgency operations and combating drug trafficking. Through specialized training, the U.S. has helped build a well-equipped and skilled Colombian military force capable of effectively countering these threats.

Financial aid has also been instrumental in empowering Colombian counter-narcotics operations. The U.S. has allocated substantial resources to support the Colombian government's efforts to interdict drug shipments, dismantle drug cartels, and disrupt money laundering networks associated with drug trafficking. These funds have enabled the Colombian law enforcement agencies to enhance their capabilities in drug interdiction and intelligence gathering.

Moreover, the U.S. has extended financial assistance for programs focused on drug addiction prevention and treatment. Recognizing that addressing the demand side of the drug problem is equally important, the U.S. has supported Colombian initiatives aimed at reducing drug addiction rates and providing rehabilitation services to those affected.

In addition to direct military support, the U.S. has aided Colombian efforts in border security and drug trafficking prevention. Assistance in the form of technology, intelligence sharing, and joint operations has bolstered Colombia's ability to secure its borders and prevent the entry and exit of illicit drugs and insurgent groups.

Recognizing the importance of economic development in tackling the root causes of drug trafficking and insurgency, the U.S. has provided financial aid for programs focused on alternative livelihoods and economic development in regions affected by these issues. By promoting sustainable economic opportunities, these initiatives aim to provide viable alternatives to individuals involved in drug trafficking and support the overall stability and prosperity of affected regions.

In conclusion, the U.S. has taken a comprehensive approach in supporting Colombia's efforts to combat drug trafficking and insurgent groups. Through military training, financial aid, and support for various programs, the U.S. has been actively engaged in addressing the multifaceted challenges faced by Colombia. This collaboration between the U.S. and Colombia serves as an example of effective cooperation in the fight against drug trafficking and insurgency, and the positive impact it has had on the security and development of Colombia.

www.ingramcontent.com/pod-product-compliance
Lightning Source LLC
Chambersburg PA
CBHW031136160726
47987CB00026B/902